CAN'T LET GO

PART TWO:

THE
HIDDEN AGENDA

ALSO BY CC FANN

CAN'T LET GO PART ONE

CAN'T LET GO PART ONE: THE TESTIMONIAL

COMMON SENSE: DO NOT PLAY THE GAME WITH AN INMATE

CAN'T LET GO PART TWO: THE HIDDEN AGENDA THE TESTIMONIAL

YOU CAN ORDER THESE TITLES FROM

WWW.CCFANN.NET OR
WWW.CCFANNCOMMONSENSE.COM
JABS PUBLICATIONS, LLC
P. O. BOX 81
WRIGHTSVILLE, GA 31096

CAN'T LET GO

PART TWO:

THE HIDDEN AGENDA

BY CC FANN

Published by JABS PUBLICATIONS

Copyright © 2008 by CC Fann

All rights reserved, which includes the right to reproduce this book or portions thereof in any form whatsoever except as provided by the U.S. Copyright law.

ISBN: 9781598724592

Text and Composition: Asta Publications, LLC

PUBLISHER'S NOTE

This book is a work of fiction. Names, characters, places, and incidents either are the product of the author's imagination or are used fictitiously, and any resemblance to actual persons, living or dead business establishments, events, or locales is entirely coincidental.

Without limiting the rights under copyright reserved above, no part of this publication may be reproduced, stored in or introduced into a retrieval system, or transmitted, in any form, or by any means(electronic, mechanical, photocopying, recording, or otherwise), without the prior written permission of both the copyright owner and the above publisher of this book.

The scanning, uploading, and distribution of this book via the Internet or via any other means without the permission of the publisher is illegal and punishable by law. Please purchase only authorized electronic editions, and do not participate in or encourage electronic piracy of copyright materials. Your support of the author's right is appreciated While the author's has made every effort to provide accurate telephone numbers and Internet addresses at the time of publication, neither the publisher nor the author assumes any responsibility for errors, or for changes that occur after publication. Further, the publisher does not have any control over and does not assume any responsibility for author or third-party Web sites or their content.

Printed in the United States of America

No matter what, don't let fears, rejection, denial, what someone may think of you and/or even say about you stop you. If you ever have a dream, idea, or goal, don't let anything stop you. It took me all of my life to get over the fear. Don't let it take you this long. I know now only you can stop yourself.

—CC Fann

Failure is when you allow manmade obstacles, such as their decisions, stop you and you settle and do not try again. But First Corinthians states that no eye has seen, no ear has heard, and no mind has imagined what God has prepared for those who love Him. So until God stops you try, try, and try again.

—CC Fann

Letter From The Author

First, let me thank my Lord, Father, Jesus Christ, My Savior and My God, for without Him there would not be a me.

Yes, I am back at it again. Taking you down the road of McKenzie Scott's life. Someone asked me how real is she. Well, she is very real. I created McKenzie Scott to teach lessons of the heart, especially to single women. The reason for the five-part series is that I wanted to talk about the different relationships that single women become involved in. Why, for some reasons, they can't let go, no matter how bad a relationship is.

In the first part, if you are woman who dated someone's husband, you are McKenzie Scott. You are a woman who put a man before your children and God. You are McKenzie. If you are a woman who knows that the relationship you are in is a dead end, you are McKenzie Scott.

I often tell married women before they read the book that this is a book for them as well. God dealt with McKenzie for dating this man, but remember—it takes two to do wrong or commit adultery.

In Part 1, there were a lot of hidden messages, but I wonder how many readers found these messages and learned from them. Did you just judge her by her actions?

Part 2, The Hidden Agenda, will take you on another path of relationships. Why do we choose to live with a man and not get married? I ask you. Please see the hidden agenda in this book. Just as in Can't Let Go, there are events or lessons that women have experienced. The Hidden Agenda will point out more events and lessons about life when we are dealing with relationships. Enjoy this path down another road.

Remember this is a fictional count-learn from this message.

CC FANN

Introduction

As you know already from Part 1, I like to keep it real. I like to go down dirt roads that have not been traveled in a long time. Those dirt roads that you think keep the secrets that we don't want to talk about or don't want anyone to find out about. The things we are really ashamed about. I like talking about these things because you can learn from mistakes. There are lessons to be learned in all mistakes. If you touch fire and it is hot, you can best believe it will still be hot when you touch it again.

When do we turn our lives over to Jesus? We decide OK, everything is in the past. Instead of dwelling on things in the past, we really need to learn from them. But *my people* will not let anything go, even if you forget how treacherous and scandalous you may have been.

With that, let me explain my people. I believe there are two types of people in a race. Folks and People.

Folks—Black or White—don't support you, no matter how good you are trying to be. They always find the negative in a situation. If a sister or brother comes up in life, they will say "about time," especially if it looks as if she or he got it going on. They will even make up a lie. They will say, "She is sleeping with someone's husband or prostituting." They will even say her significant other is a drug dealer. Folks can't wait for an individual to fall.

People—Black or White—encourage you. They often tell you avenues or give you advice so you can do better. They will take the time to help you. It is not about getting paid. They just want to see someone make or have the best out of life. They don't care how you do it. They do not pass judgment on you.

Right about now, I am so tired of people being ashamed of their past mistakes. As a rhythm and blues song from the '70s went, let's put it out in the open. The old cliché states that what is done in the dark will come out in the light. It was in the light already. You were just the last one to know that it was in the light.

The Hidden Agenda. I can't lie. There are a few times I have had a few hidden agendas. Whether it's good or bad, one thing you need in this day and time is a back-up plan, a Plan B, and sometimes a spare tire wouldn't help, either.

But one thing you need for sure is to make sure in any relationship you are both in the same game. It is a damn shame to be playing basketball and he is running track somewhere. When I was growing up, I watched great prime-time black TV shows, like *Good Times, The Jeffersons,* and *The Cosby Show.* What we saw in these shows was how family is to stay together. There were no hidden agendas portrayed on these TV shows. You did not see George cheat on Weezy, James cheat on Florida, and you *know* Cliff did not cheat on Claire. So what's up now? Why do men and women cheat?

The M-Connection (Moria, Maxine, Monica, Mona, and me, McKenzie) are best friends. When we were gathered at the salon getting ready for the wedding today, we debated on the perfect man and family. . We all felt the need to reminisce on my past. Mona always takes the Christian route. She said women need to stop asking the Lord for a man. Openly reliving a recent encounter, I said to her, "I know that's right because I asked God for a man and I got John. I know the Lord didn't send me John." Mona always stays in my behind. She said, "God knows you ain't right, McKenzie, and I don't know who sent John. I do believe God knows you ain't right yet, McKenzie. That's why you didn't found the right man. You needed to stop faking, putting up fronts, and, last but not least, stop being under cover." She said, "See, you are like most women, you want the wedding and the wedding cake, but not the husband. You are gonna meet your match."

"Yeah," I replied, "remember Darius?" My best friends and I couldn't help but laugh. I said, "I do not want to talk about Darius. I have already told you about Michael." Monica, who is the quiet one, said, "I want to hear about John. I didn't know you then, McKenzie." But I told her I didn't want to talk about any of them. Then Moria said, "Look, McKenzie, you can't change the past, so spill it. I have two more heads to finish before we get our nails done. Besides, the wedding is not until six o'clock. So spill it, McKenzie."

I looked at them and said all right, and Maxine said, "Wait! I need to microwave my popcorn." "At eight o'clock in the morning?" I asked. She said, "Yes, popcorn. McKenzie, these stories should be a movie."

Chapter 1

You know how you have some juicy gossip to tell? When you opened up your cell phone and you went down the directory to find anyone or someone to call? I mean some *good* juicy gossip. Gossip that I don't care whether you are dead or alive, old and young, you have to tell it.

Folks will always remember the past, especially the bad things. I don't care if you got saved and dipped in the same water that John the Baptist was dipped in. They will not forget the bad things that happened in the past.

I almost skipped writing this book to tell you about this nice nasty rascal. You do know what "nice nasty" is, don't you? It's people who are nice in the public, but nasty behind closed doors. I can't wait to tell you how I wasted five years of my life with the Devil. For real. See, a real Devil goes to church faithfully and then he lives two separate lives. My pastor would say *the saint turns into an ain't*.

The *ain't* can stand at the altar and come up with real tears. You know when the pastor is in the pulpit ending his sermon? He begins to whoop. You already know he is getting ready to whoop—when he stops teaching and begins speaking the words like he is singing. He sounds like he has asthma at the end of every sentence. There is one favorite story all preachers like to tell. It is the day that Jesus was hung on the cross between two thieves, and they buried him alone in an empty tomb. Don't let us forget how long the preacher preaches on how Jesus arose from the dead. I don't care how many times they tell that story. People get out of their seats and start praising the Lord like no other time. The House of the Lord gets crunk and has a Holy Ghost party.

Now if you are a reverend or a preacher or a pastor, and you can't get your church crunk with that sermon, something is wrong.

At the end, the preacher loves to ask how many would like to get right with the Lord while you still have a chance. He also says, "I know there is one who is battling with some personal things. I am not asking you to tell it to me. I am asking you to tell it to the Lord. You don't know when the end is near." While he is speaking, John is sitting beside me, bent over, his hands gathered in his lap, rocking back and forth preparing himself for the show. He always says, "I am sorry," very loud as he works up the tears.

I know at that moment. The show is beginning.

I look around to see who is looking at us. Just as I put my hand on his shoulder, he decides to stand up and cry to the Lord, "Lord, please help me." I am looking at him out the side of my eye like, *What is wrong with you?* As the ushers move hastily toward him, he starts walking toward the altar. Now the preacher is saying, "If there is anyone who desires prayer, please come forth." He already asked, "If you want to join the church, please come forth." Since we were visiting and were already faithful members at our own churches, I knew he wasn't talking to us. We both were happy with our home churches.

Apparently, no one wants to join today. No one comes forth.

Once John gets to the altar, he starts to do a two-step, like he's in the club. He also is waving his hands in the air. I think, if somebody yells, "Scream," he might scream and drop it like it is hot, since he looks like he is doing the electric slide. The usher is trying to get hold of him without getting hit. One poor lady is trying to get his glasses, and two more have surrounded him like they are on the school yard playing ring around the roses. He even has an usher wiping his face with some cheap Kleenex. It is leaving lint all over his face, and being dark black, he doesn't need that to happen. I am praying and asking the Lord to please get this over without sending down lightning, thunder, hurricanes, and tornadoes.

The preacher is praying, and when someone hollers out, he prays harder. I stand up at my seat, patiently doing my silent prayer and thanking the Lord for everything—life, health, strength. I also thank him for my children, my four beautiful angels.

But my first prayer is asking the Lord to get me out of this relationship safely. After the prayer is over, John returns to his seat beside me, escorted by the ushers. As he comes near me, he doesn't have his glasses on, and he inadvertently looks up to see who is looking before he sits down. Just in case anyone is looking, he would scream again and bend at the knees as if he was going to collapse.

I notice everyone is looking to see if I am going to comfort him or even wipe his face. In my mind, I say, *Hell, no!* Yes, I am in the church, but the Lord knows I'm not a fake. So I play it off, pat him on the knee, and make gestures that everything is going to be all right.

I played this role every time we went to church. I knew what was going to happen when we drove off the church ground. Just like my pastor said, *the saint turns into an ain't.*

I know you are going to curse me out for what I am about to say next. Read the next book. I am going to really step on some fake church folks' toes.

Chapter 2

I thought I had it going on, as you already know. Despite what Mona said, I was real as it gets. Mona was married for fifteen years and never knew what it was like to be a single mother, but I was just not into allowing my kids to become part of damage control in any relationship. So, yes, I was being fake. Fake was good because no matter how badly I wanted a man in my bed at night, I just could not do it because of not disrespecting my kids.

I was into wearing weaves. If you can't grow it, sew it, if you believe it, weave it, and if you buy it, glue it. So I didn't mind wearing someone else's hair or animal hair, as long as I looked good. My body was tight. I had a great job. On my job, I was one of the only two blacks working in administration. I had a little *edumacation*. I was the shit. I tried to stay grounded, but I could not help but toot my own horn from time to time. I wore stylish clothes.

After I got rid of that devil John, he left me well off. During the separation I never paid for hair, nails, or clothes. When I made an effort to give him all his merchandise back, he wouldn't accept it. See, the Devil wouldn't buy me anything out of Goody's or Cato's. Oh, no. He wanted me to wear Macy's, Belk's, and JC Penny. Which in our world were the rich folks' stores.

I didn't miss the Devil, but I did miss all those benefits. But what good is it all if I am dead? I set out to find another John, but not a crazy one.

I came off my horse and went slumming. I went on date after date. I was bound and determined to find someone to out-do John. I heard it was written in the Player's Handbook that when you end a relationship, and the person was classified as a Toyota Corolla, you go up and get the next level. They need to be a Toyota Camry. If you work it right, you may get a Lexus. But please don't get a Pinto. They don't even make replacement parts for Pintos anymore.

After I didn't have any success, I decided to get me a man that wasn't attractive but hard working. One that didn't socialize with a lot people but who stayed to himself. Remember the rules. The children had to like him. You do remember the rules in Book 1? Well, if you don't remember the rules and don't have a copy of the book, because you borrowed it from someone, well, I don't think they are going to let you borrow it twice. Guess what—I am not going to recite the rules again.
.

Chapter 3

The first time we met, I was in training at Powell State Prison. He was also an employee. He was assigned to the special task force and could access any area of the institution without being questioned about it. When the instructor let us have a break, he appeared. There he was, standing there with a cute smile. I didn't see a wedding band. Nothing to brag about, I thought. He'll do just fine. He wasn't the best thing to look at, I thought, so I should not have to worry about him running around. Maybe nobody else would want him.

Speaking of a wedding band, the legislature needs to pass a law for all people who are married. They need to wear a wedding band. If caught without one, they need to do a year of community service. It should be called GC A, Section 66-04-911 in the felony laws. Married women dog out all of us single women about going out with their husbands, and they can't even make them wear their wedding bands?

They have the nerve to call us single women scandalous. They call us whores and anything and everything else except our real names. They even say we should know our place. Hell, we do know. *Your husband just want to know our place, too.* When I was married, I didn't say anything to those sluts he was cheating with. I put my foot in his ass. When he didn't do right after two strikes, I left. There was no use to wait on the third strike and get put out coming into home. I left. I was like Jed Clampett in *The Beverly Hillbillies*. I loaded up the truck and moved to the projects.

How do we as single women know when we are at the clubs if a man is married or not? It is not like you can go in the club and ask the deejay to pull up some man's bio. What needs to happen is a married man needs to wear one of those ankle bracelets. When they have cheating thoughts, the bracelet will send electrical shocks through their bodies.

Especially, if they look at another person, whether it is man or woman. Please forgive me. I am sorry. I had to vent.

Married people always get us single people in trouble. But I can't talk for all single people. Just the ones who are trying to do right.

After talking with Darius Howard on a few occasions, I decided it was time to check the NCIC. The NCIC on our job. Check to see if you have any warrant or criminal activity in the past. The street committee's definition of NCIC is *Negro Control Investigative Channel*. See, if you're a Negro that is a dog and has three different baby mommies, the NCIC has registered you as baby momma drama man. Be a wife beater, don't pay any bills, but take care of your kids—the NCIC has got you. It has you even if you are a deadbeat dad who does pay child support. See, the channel is so powerful that all you need to do is make one call. That is all. The NCIC will give a report of you, your family tree, what kind of job you have, your marriage history, and how many kids you have and by who.

Now what you do with this information is strictly up to the subscriber.

But just like the surgeon general, the NCIC has a warning. *This information may result in death or be hazardous to your health. Please proceed with caution.*

See, the NCIC had given me the printout on Darius Howard. Everything looked good, except he was separated from his wife, not divorced. He had two girls by two different women, which he took care of to the fullest. I thought I might take this another step further. I hoped NCIC was not wrong, because some brothers know how to beat the system and slip through the cracks.

I just had to get by that he was not that attractive, even though he was a hard worker. I know what you're thinking. You're thinking I must think I am all that and then some. Yes, I did. I was very conceited. Appearance and status meant a lot. I had worked hard for it. If you know what I had been through in my first marriage, you wouldn't ask. That is Book 4.

Chapter 4

I know we should never judge the book by its cover. I just wanted the cover to look good. I must take a chapter to tell you why I decided to date someone that was not so attractive.

See, back in the day, I would hear the older sisters say everybody wants a pretty boy. He needs to be light skinned and have good hair, so more than likely your baby will look good, too. The only problem was these kinds of men will not keep a job. They are too pretty to work. Then the pretty-boy, light-skinned brothers' stock went down. The only value they had was they could make pretty babies, and sometimes that didn't work out, either. I have seen some ugly light-skinned babies in my day.

But the sisters wised up and said, *I'm not sharing. Give me an ugly, dark-skinned brother that don't mind getting dirty on the job.* They figured it out. *I can dress him up in a FUBA outfit and a pair of ADIDAS, and he will look just as good.* FUBA stands for *For Ugly Brother Association.*

One of my childhood friends dated this light-skinned brother. She was just strung out about him, and he cheated on her with everybody. She was miserable. So she vowed she would never date another light-skinned brother again. Now keep in mind, she was light-skinned with long hair down her back. She was popular, captain of the cheerleader squad, Homecoming Princess.

One Monday we all were eating lunch and doing our usual gossiping at the senior table. She said she was bringing her new man to the game on Friday. We all were like that Heinz Ketchup commercial. ANTICIPATION. We were waiting for more information, but nothing came until she was ready to tell us. The event was Friday. All week long, we could not wait to meet him and see what he looked like. She would constantly say he was an ugly black Negro with a good job and he treated her like a queen.

The night of the football game, we all were walking back and forth to the concession stand, trying to pick him out of the crowd before halftime. We had our skittles ready. We often took skittles, those candies that look like M & M's but had an S on them. The bag had every color of the rainbow, just like the commercial said. It was our way of letting each other knows that someone was ugly or had on an ugly outfit. It was an inside joke. We would say this would get the bitter taste out of our mouth.

The color red rated the highest, as being the ugliest. The green skittle meant he was fine. Each color had its own definition.

It was a hot, humid night in August, the first football game of the season, and we were trying to get a sneak preview before she introduced him. Being a cheerleader, she could not visit with us until halftime.

Being nomales (meaning *nosy females*), we were on our job. I saw one guy. He was so ugly, he had on a two piece, light orange, polyester suit with bell bottoms. I prayed before I looked down because I knew this Negro would not have on high heel stacks in the '80s. Guess what. He did. I asked, *When did John Travolta turn black and ugly?* I had not seen *Saturday Night Fever* in six years, and I was hoping I was not having flashback. Did this man think we were still in the '70s? I knew he was hot with that wannabe imitation silk/polyester shirt. He was black and the shirt was black, and the only way you knew he had on the shirt because it had big white and yellow flowers on it. Then he had an afro when everyone was wearing curly kits. I knew he had to be here with the visiting team.

I frowned up and ate a skittle. He was so ugly, I could taste it. Then I ate another piece of candy, just to get the taste out of my mouth. I pointed him out to my friends when he almost broke his ass with those high heels he had on. My friends and I had a field day laughing at him.

Then we saw another guy who looked like he had just got off of work. He wasn't that good looking. He had on a blue mechanic's overall covered in grease. *We knew that was him.* We bumped into him on purpose. We even tried to strike up a conversation, but he didn't give us any information. We knew this was our man. He was trying to be stuck up but not disrespectful. Finally, we gave up and walked away.

We were standing there, looking silly and cursing her out for making us wait to see the man, and my friend Chris said, "I hoped he is something to look at." I said, "Yeah. I wonder what."

Then Liesa came up to us and told us to turn around, she would be right back with her date. You would think we were trying to go out with the man, too, we were so anxious. And I hated surprises.

She came back and told us to close our eyes and then turn around. I was always the stubborn one. I wanted to be first. Instead of closing my eyes, I held my head down so she could not see my eyes open. I did this the way Jamie Fox on *Living Color* played the part of Wanda. He played a transvestite. Wanda would always look at other people from the feet up to their head. This way she could analyze, dissect, and give them what she thought of them all in one breath. If you know any homosexuals, you know they love looking at you from the feet up to your head when they check you out.

I turned around. I saw those shoes. I closed my eyes and ate another skittle. Then Liesa bumped me and said, "You can open your eyes, McKenzie." I said, "I think I got a bug in them." I ran to the bathroom because I was afraid my mouth would get me in trouble. I was too through.

While I was in the bathroom, I prayed a prayer for forgiveness. I was about to sin. I was going back out there and be polite, courteous, and respectful after I had dogged his bad dressing Kunta Kinte-looking ass out. I splashed some water on my face to look like I had washed my eyes and ate another skittle. I knew Liesa was trying to make a point, but I thought she'd gone too far.

When I arrived back at the group, I was amazed to see how fake and phony we were. Because he was there alone, we offered to let him sit with us until the end of the game. But as ugly as he was, he was nice and mannerly. Liesa looked at him like he was Denzel Washington.

I had to give her respect, though. She was not ashamed. She was happy. She made me change my opinion. Instead of looking for the popular, good-looking guys after that occasion, I dated guys that were not popular. There is a catch to this, though. When you bring them out and dress them up, everybody wants them! Keep that little note in mind.

Chapter 5

Darius would often call me. My son, who thought he was the man of the house, would always answer. I don't know what they talked about, but my son would always be grinning from ear to ear. I tried to get him to tell me what they were talking about, but my own child would not tell me. I have always tried to satisfy my kids when I was dating. If the kids didn't like him, he had to go.

Anyway, I finally decided to go on a date with Darius. As a matter of fact, we went on several dates. I wanted to do this before I decide to let him meet the children. This time, I was cooking dinner for him and the kids. When he drove up in his beat-up car, Cameron flew outside to meet him. My sons never like anyone I had dated before, especially that drama queen, John, so they happily escorted Darius in. I watched and listen as they conversated.

Our home was a very small two-bedroom single trailer. I had to move from the projects when I got my state job because living in the projects is based on your income, and I was not going to pay $400 a month when my neighbors pay $11. The projects were good when I was on welfare and going to school to further my education, but I couldn't stay, so when I got my state job, I thanked them for everything and moved out. My rent for this trailer was $165. I only had lights, telephone, and gas to pay, no cable or satellite, which hadn't made it in the country yet, anyway. I was satisfied with CBS, NBC, and ABC because all the TV and games in my house usually go off at nine p.m. The TV was off even when we ate dinner. I have to enforce good quality family time. It means so much when you grow old and you want to remember the good old days.

We were blessed to have a large front yard and a back yard. Even though I lived in a trailer, I hated trailers with a passion. I always reminded myself this was *temporary*. How many times do you see on the news and hear all the bad things about living in trailers? How people would burn up due to the windows being too small to get out? They report that the exterior buckled from the heat and melted.

My worst nightmare was if a tornado would come through and hit our trailer. It was scary, thinking about me in the kids flying through the air like Dorothy in *The Wizard of Oz*. Tornadoes always seem to hit trailer parks. The way the news shows the tornado, it picks up the trailer, spins it around, and throws it a distance, spreading everything that was in the trailer into the woods. If the tornado doesn't pick it up, the lack of oxygen will make the trailer buckle and explode.

Every time bad weather comes, I don't gather my belongings and go to someone else's home. I say a prayer and go to sleep. I leave everything in the Lord's hand. Who's to say that the tornado won't get me while I am trying to go somewhere else?

I could never understand my grandmother, who also lives in a trailer. She would cut off all the electricity, shut the windows, and go to my sister, who lives in a trailer, too. They would sit over there in the dark until the weather passed. Tornadoes usually come in the summer months, and it was hot as hell in that trailer. I knew it was. I told my grandmother, a trailer is a trailer. A tornado does not discriminate which trailer it will hit.

With all that knowledge of what will happen, you still see trailers being sold every day or being pulled to someone's land.

Chapter 6

Darius made himself comfortable. He didn't judge me because of my living arrangements, at least he didn't act like he did. Three kids sleeping in one room wasn't functional, not to mention we had clothes for days, and there were boxes in every corner. But it was clean. There were no rats and roaches. He asked me what the boxes were for. I stated I had always dreamed of building a house. I had started buying my wall decorations for each room. I already had new furniture in storage that I will furnish the house with. "I am saving money to put down to build a house in country," I said. All he could say was, "That is interesting."

He also noticed I am a collector. I collect Barbie dolls for my daughter, collectible cars and any type baseball or basketball cards for the boys. As long as it says collector or special edition, I collect it. I especially love antique furniture.

It was Friday. Hamburger and French fries night for the kids. Darius was always asking me to go out and eat, so I decided to ask him did he want to join us in a family meal. You have to observe how a man interacts with your kids, especially if you want to keep him around for a while.

Josh and Cameron seemed to enjoy his company, but Sean was a little hesitant, though later he was okay. I knew if there was anyone to please, it would be Cameron. Cameron doesn't like any man that tries to talk to his mommy. He's too grown up for his own good. "Mommy," he tells me, "they just want somewhere they can lay up and don't have to pay bills. They all are just free loaders. Not me," he says. "I plan to marry and take care of my wife and kids." I knew Cameron hated his dad. He blamed him for all the hard times we have had.

No one could understand how could a man have potential great athletes and good students as children and then not want to be a part of his children's lives. It was just sad. All kids want to see their dads sitting in the stands as they play sports. It just makes it more worthwhile to a child. That is why you hardly see professional athletes recognize their dads. It is always I bought my momma a house. That should let you know. If he has a dad, the dad may stay in the house, but that is all. He can't make any claim on the house if anything happens.

After dinner, everyone seemed pleased and we all sat down and watched TV together. After awhile, Josh gave hints to his siblings that it was time to go to bed. He was being polite, trying to give Darius and me some alone time. But Cameron didn't get the hint. Cameron said, "Mom, can I talk to you about something before I go to bed?" "Cameron," I said back to him, "what is it you want to talk about?" He began to rattle off something. Then Josh called out and told him his bed felt wet. I knew Josh was lying. But Cameron flew down the hallway. I heard some tussling, and then everything was quiet.

It felt good having Darius in our home. He was very attentive, especially to me. He was a great conversationalist and loved talking about his kids. In the end, our home date went very well.

I knew that eventually I could not make any excuses about coming home from a date to get the kids to avoid having sex.

Chapter 7

I was sitting at my desk when my co-worker, Chastity, told me that I had flowers at the front building. I knew John was world famous for sending me flowers. I hoped Darius wouldn't find out about the flowers, but I knew this was impossible. I didn't budge. I told her, "I will get them when I leave for the day." But she was so fast and nosy; she walked her big behind to the front and picked them up for me.

Chastity and I worked side by side in the counseling department. She was the first white woman I ever saw that had a black woman figure. She had a little waist and a big ass. She made me insecure about my shape. I am not a lesbian, but you couldn't help but look. It was just how her body was made. It just made you look. She had pale white skin with a Dolly Parton hairstyle.

But believe me, she must had some black in her, because she loved to flaunt her body off. Every day, all kinds of white men stopped by our office and made gestures. Black men stopped by, too. Some even came bearing gifts. I loved it when they came. Some weeks, I didn't have to worry about lunch because they treated both us to lunch. The sad things about her, at least for them, was she wasn't giving up any ass. She said she loved her husband.

The problem was she just loves flirting. She leads them on often. I have told her repeatedly she is writing a check her ass can't cash. When someone comes by, or a man in particular, she has to get up and walk to the file cabinet to get a file. My all-time favorite is when she drops something and has to pick it up. I love watching how the white guy's face turns red when he watches her behind. I know they know I'm watching to see how they react. They try to hold their composure.

Chastity would ask them to come in just to see what type of reaction their d*** was doing. Believe me, some reactions didn't register a

2 on the Richter scale when they had an erection. We would just laugh because she said she was not sleeping with a man who didn't have a big d***. If they didn't outdo her husband, they needed to find another victim.

When Chastity returned from the front building, she gave me a dozen gorgeous white roses trimmed in orange. The card read, You are cordially invited to a full night of dancing, dinner, and pampering. I want to spoil you for a night by any means necessary on Friday. In the card was a hundred dollar bill and another note saying, Get your hair done and buy something nice to wear to bed. Love, Darius.

I had to be like the black folks. I've got plenty to wear to bed. What I need is an outfit to go out in. I said, "I guess I am supposed to go out naked." Chastity laughed and said, "That will save you some money to buy an outfit for bed. You will already be in your birthday suit." I told her, kiss my ass. Chastity said, "Darius is going to kiss more than your ass on Friday. Quit trying to appear hard. You know that man bought you some roses, gave you a hundred dollar bill, and is taking you out for dinner and dancing. You know you got to give up some ass. You need some good sex." She asked me, "How long has it been? A year?"

She said, "You said it yourself. It is hard to find a man, and I quote, a good black man who wants to date a woman with four kids." She said, "Hell, I would not date a man with one kid. Live a little. At least you got a hundred dollars out of the deal, and you are still single. You can date whoever you want. How you are going to find a man if you don't date? Don't let Dr. Phil fool you. They did not have online dating when he found his wife. If my husband sent me some roses, I would leave work find his ass and fuck him all night. Okay?"

Chastity had a point. I called Darius and I accepted his invitation.

Chapter 8

There was no need to make a hair appointment because Moria had just done my hair on Saturday, and I had plenty of outfits for the bed. The Devil stayed in Victoria's Secret, buying me outfits all the time. I knew this would be nasty. Wearing what someone else bought you. But guess what—the Devil is not going to see it again. Why let it go to waste? I picked out several outfits. How would Darius know if I didn't buy them? I'll just deposit that money in my saving account and plan to wear something I already had in my lingerie drawer. I was planning to match what he might wear to bed.

Like Chastity, I had been checking out his merchandise whenever he hugged me close. He seemed average. I hoped he was average, anyway. Above average is a dream come true. He has so much potential. But if he is below average, I guess we have to work with it. But nowadays, *size don't count*. It is how you use it. Men, if you can work it right, women will come back for more.

He sent a limo to pick me up. I knew my mom was looking out her window. I could see her saying, *What in the hell is a limo doing on a dirt road at a single wide trailer? My child knows she can find some fools. What fool would be stupid enough to spend that kind of money for that? The money he spent on a limo, he needs to buy groceries, pay the light and gas bills. Hell, he can buy me groceries if he wants to. I need some money, too. Lord, what will men do for some ass?*

As I was sitting in the limo, I noticed more roses. The limo had a bar with red wine and chocolate-covered cherries. I knew this was probably just a one-time fantasy that I will live, so I planned to make the best of it. If it means getting my freak on, that's what I will do. But to me, it's the little things that count, not riding in a big limo.

When I arrived at the restaurant, there he was, standing in front wearing a black shirt and tan slacks with a black leather sport blazer. And holding more roses. I had a big-ass smile on my face that would make Ronald McDonald look like he was frowning. He looked so sexy. This was the first time I had seen him wearing this type of apparel.

As I stepped out, he was checking me out from head to toe. I knew he liked what he saw. I was wearing a simple, black silk, halter-top dress that clung to my body and matching three-inch heels that strapped up midway my leg. Everyone has a dress that you wear when you want to reveal your assets or one that does the body good. This dress definite did that in the cleavage department. My skin was silky smooth, thanks to Johnson & Johnson Baby Oil. It glowed under the stars. To prove that he liked what he saw, he asked could we skip dinner. But, being a lady, I declined and said, "Eat first. We have all night for anything else." He said, That's what I want to do, is eat." I smiled, trying to look innocent. It was a beautiful night.

He had preordered dinner. He ordered us one-inch steaks smothered with onions and mushrooms, with small red potatoes on the side. For dessert, he surprised me with a chocolate fudge cupcake sitting in the middle of vanilla ice cream. The top of the cupcake read, in white frosting *More To Come*. That when I felt really anxious. What else could he do to make this night better?

What does this man have up his sleeve? I hope this is not the last supper. I hope he is not Dr. Jekyll and Mr. Hyde. I mean, after the night, he won't even remember my name or he'll ignore me for whatever reasons. But for the moment, I did not care. I was being treated like a diva.

After dinner, we went dancing at the local jazz bar, O'Brian's. It was a cozy, quiet bar with a live band that did great renditions of contemporary jazz. Our first dance was to the saxophone soloist playing Luther Vandross's "If This World Was Mine." Darius ordered champagne with cherries in it, and after he finished the drink, he began to eat the cherry slowly. After he finished the cherry, he placed the stem in his mouth and said, "Let me show you something." Somehow, he tied the cherry stem in a nice little bow with his tongue.

This arouses me so much that I almost open my legs right there in the club. I tell him I'm not feeling well and ask can we leave early. He says sure, with a smile. He knows what he has done. He knows the effect he had on me with the cherry stem.

If he can perform that kind of feat with a cherry stem, I'm wondering what else he can do with his tongue. My mind is definitely slumming in the gutter.

Chapter 9

When we arrive in front of the Marriott, I'm stunned. "Are we staying here tonight?" I ask him. He says yes. I say, "This place is expensive. Shoot, the price for one night alone is probably my rent. You could have given me the money," I add, "and we could have stayed home. The kids are not there tonight." He says, "Nothing but the best for my woman."

Apparently he has checked in already, because we go straight to the elevator. When the elevator stops on the sixth floor, he asks, "Are you ready?" "Yes," I say. When we enter the room, I am amazed at the candles and more flowers. They are everywhere. He holds me close and gives me a box. "Just in case you were being cheap and didn't buy something for the bedroom, I decided to buy you something that I know no one has seen." "Damn," I say. *This Negro must have surveillance equipment on my ass somewhere.* I grin and say to him, "I just wasted good money and time looking for the perfect outfit for you, and you bought me an outfit." I'm lying my ass off, as you know.

He nudges me to the bathroom to change. "Please, go change." I go into the bathroom. This is a man that knows what he wants. Inside the box are a thin, black, two-piece thong with bra, a sheer jacket, thigh highs and shoes with five-inch glass heels. After assembling this outfit on my body, I look like I'm in one of those video flicks. I must admit I look damn good, but I'm so nervous, I feel like a hooker in church. I'm trying to figure out how to make an entrance from the bathroom without making a fool out of myself.

I guess he could not wait. I hear a knock on the door asking me do I need help. I reply no and open the door. He grabs me by the waist and pulls me close. He almost startles me, he's so aggressive. As he slowly begins kissing me, he picks me up and walks toward the bed. He lays me down in the middle of bed and stands over me, observing the out fit. "Just perfect," he says. "I knew you would look perfect." He walks to the foot of the bed and pulls off his pajama top. He says, "Now let me show you how I tied the cherry stem."

He kneels before me and opens my legs. My anticipation is so great, I know I won't be able to handle what he's going to do to me. It's been seven months. The first touch of his tongue makes me scream. I'm already moist. He uses that to his advantage. It has been a long time since anyone has kiss and/or licked on my womanhood. If he doesn't stop, I'll pass out.

After I have my second orgasm, he stops and looks at me and says, "Now let me give you that massage." I say, as if I was a real ghetto chick from the projects, "I know you are gonna finish this. As a might of fact you need to finish this now. I need you inside of me now." "No," he says, smiling, "no, you need to wait." "I'll just be damned, I say. I still haven't seen what he is working with. When he asks me to turn over, I just go with it. The massage is great, but my womanhood is mad as hell and it lets me know by feeling like it was on fire.

He says, "You are very tense." I say, "It has been a long day." I am thinking to myself, *You'd be tense, too, if you knew my hormones was having a nervous breakdown since you got them so hot and bothered.* Then he says, "Let me give you something to take the edge off." I think he is getting up to get me a drink, but he lies on the back of me and slips himself inside of me. I moan out loud, it is so good and unbelievable. It's a dream come true, how he made love to me. I have a brother in the bed with a nice tool and it is mine for the taking. I took all of it, inch by inch.

It was a competition between us. I had to make him pay for making me wait so long. He was definitely what I needed. For the next two hours, we were in a marathon, there was no position or act he could do that I could not compete with. I was ready for anything and every position he had except one; the cherry stem maneuver, the one that started this marathon. When he placed his head between my legs, I surrendered like any army does when it is outnumbered. I was glad to be a prisoner tonight.

Chapter 10

After a great night, we had breakfast in bed, with which he had his own personal dessert, which was me. It was a night to remember. I didn't want to be negative, but I had to prepare myself mentally for what would happen in the days to come. I had to be pessimistic, just in case I didn't hear from him again. When someone goes out like he did and makes you feel like royalty, you can't help but think, *Who all he has treated this way?* Or, *Did I impress him enough that he will keep spoiling me?* Anyway, after all the contemplating, I gave up to the idea I'd had a good time. I could not wait to tell my friends what happened. Except the cherry stem maneuver.

Once I got home and got the kids settled in, he must have known I needed assurance. He called and said how good a time he had and he wanted to do it again. Feeling a little giddy, I asked, did he want to come over and watch TV. I was scared to death that he would say no, but he said yes and he would bring some popcorn and drinks. Yessss. I hung up.

I couldn't wait to see him. When he arrived and made himself comfortable, he whispered in my ear, "Last night was your night. Tonight is the kids' night." I felt a little jealous. But I knew if you want a man, a good man, and you have kids, he needs to spend time with your kids, too. Amen.

Family night was good. That is, until Lessie stopped by unannounced. See, I wasn't ready to introduce him to the family just yet. I wasn't hiding him or anything, but Lessie is the president of the news network in our family. By midnight tonight, everybody will know, or least they will have her side of my news story: *McKenzie Has a New Man, Again.*

She claimed she needed some sugar because she was making a cake and the store was closed. I knew that was a lie. I said we were out, I didn't have any. But Josh, with his big mouth, hollered out and said,

"Yes we do, Momma. I just made some Kool-Aid today and opened up a new bag." So, being caught up, I had no choice but to allow her to come in. I didn't even ask her to sit down. She just made herself comfortable. She was preparing herself for the interview. She knew she only had five minutes to do it before I gave her the look.

To jump off her twenty-one questions, she asked Darius, "How are you doing? Where do I know you? You look familiar. Where did you say you were from? Who did you say was your family? You must work with my daughter. Did I see you down here last week? I know where I saw you at. Were you in the National Guard? Are you related to any Bells? You favor one of my friend's children that are Bells."

Keep in mind: all Darius had said was, "How are you doing, ma'am?" And, "I am doing fine."

Instead of pouring her a cup of sugar, I gave her what was left in the bag, which was three fourths full, and I also gave her a look with an attitude that said, *Get hell out!*

Since we communicated well with the looks on our faces, she got up and tried to make one last stab by asking him to come up for Sunday dinner when he was not working. And if he had any kids, he could bring them, too. Darius smiled and said "Thank you, ma'am," and then, "Good night, ma'am."

After she was gone, I knew she was going to call back, trying to pry out some more information, so I took time out and walked through the house and turned the ringers off on all the phones. I knew that would make her mad. After the movies, it was late and the kids went to bed. I walked Darius to his truck and gave him a long kiss goodnight. It was a full moon. I should have caught the second warning.

Everybody knows when there is a full moon, there is nothing but trouble coming. Only thing good about it is, old people used to say that most babies were born during the cycle of the full moon.

I do remember in the movies, when there is a full moon that's when regular people turn in to vampires and werewolves. The evilness comes out of them. *Keep this little note in your mind for future reference.*

When I finally got into bed later on that night, I remembered and turned the ringers on the phones back on. Then I laid my head on my pillow. The phone rang. It scared the daylight out of me. It was Darius, calling to say good night. When we hung up, I thought about those werewolves and vampires. I don't believe in them, but I didn't want to take any chances. I slept with the light on, just in case.

Chapter 11

When I arrived at work on Monday morning, Chastity could not wait for the details. She had hung the sign on the office door that said, Meeting in Progress, Come Back or Call in 15 Minutes. Our supervisor doesn't report to work until nine o'clock, so we were safe. She had my favorite chocolate Krispy Kreme doughnut and a bottle of Tropicana Orange Juice sitting on my desk. She sat in front of my desk and crossed her legs and said, "Talk or die!"

She had that evil look on her face. I decided not to eat my doughnut or drink my orange juice. I planned to save them until later, just in case she had done something to my food. I tried to give her the run around, just to have fun, but she was getting a little anxious, so I finally spilled the beans. I told her play by play. She was in awe. She finally said, "Damn, girl! All that sex and you are not tired?" I said, "No, I am actually full of energy." "Well," she said, "I'm jealous. I know I'm going to get me some tonight. Just thinking about that cherry stem gets me excited, too."

Then someone knocked at the door, so we made an effort to appear like we were doing some work. It was Darius, standing there with a big-ass smile. He asked, "How are you doing?" I said, "I am doing fine." He said, "I tried to call you before you left for work to tell you to have a good day." I said, "I'm sorry, I had to leave early to take the kids to school for a field trip." Chastity said, "Do I need to leave you two alone?" "No," I said, and Darius said, "Let me know what you want for lunch. I am paying." When Chastity said, "Darius, what are you eating for lunch?" he looked at me and smiled, and she said, "I don't think they sell what you want in the local restaurant." "What do you mean?" he asked, and she said, "I mean you keep looking at McKenzie like she is on the menu." He looked like he was blushing and he said, "Girl, you are crazy." Before he could get into more trouble, he walked away and said, "I'll call you later." I picked up a pen and threw it at her. We just laughed.

After that weekend, every day we scheduled our lunch together. Darius always gave me a phone call in the morning, in the evening, and before I went to sleep at night. He also called and checked on the kids. We attended sporting events together. We were inseparable.

Meanwhile, Lessie was on the prowl. She called me to her house to help her understand some mail she had received. I was prepared to give her information about Darius, so she would be satisfied, but I didn't have time for a full interrogation.

See, Lessie, as you know from *Can't Let Go*, is good. She knows the 411, the 611, and the 911. The 411: general information, maybe good, maybe bad. The 611: stuff you wish nobody knew and wish they'd forget. You don't like using this code. But the 911 is when it is juicy and you call every time you want to know something in a hurry and get a quick response. Just like the ambulance responding to a medical emergency or a fire truck to a fire.

I knew Lessie had the 411, so right now she was waiting for any 911 she could get. Not to beat around the bush with her, I brought it up. That threw her off guard a little bit. I told her the general information, but I knew she had a card in her hand she wanted to play. I hesitated and waited for her to play it. It was like playing spades. She said, "I heard he was separated and not divorced." I said, "That is true." She said, "Well, when is he getting a divorce?" I said, "Same time you get a man." She said, "Well, I guess he won't ever marry you." I said, "I never said I wanted to marry him." Then the phone rang. That gave me an excuse to get up and leave. When I got outside, I smiled. I knew I had won that round.

I knew she meant well. She just didn't know how to do it.

Chapter 12

It was time to show him off to my friends and family. One of my classmates, who was like a brother to me, was getting married, not to mention my cousin was getting married next month, too. I had invited Darius to come along with me. I already knew he wasn't an outgoing person, but I knew if he was serious about me, he was going to go. I could not wait for everyone to meet him. I also knew John would be there. I needed to show him I had moved on. In my eyes, Darius was a good catch.

Darius was handsome in his navy blue suit, but I just could not show up in that car he was driving. Since I invited him, I offered to drive. I was blessed with two vehicles. I had just bought a new one, a Lexus 300, before the breakup with John. That was one of the benefits I kept out of that relationship. The only time I drove it was on the weekends to special functions. You know, just to show off. My work car was very reliable and still in good condition. But my Lexus 300? I never move my baby.

To let him think he was still in charge, I allowed him to drive. When we walked into the church, all eyes were on us. I could see question marks above everyone's head. *Who in the hell is that brother with her?* I smiled politely at everyone as we took our seat.

It was a beautiful ceremony and the reception was great. I took time to greet everyone and introduce Darius as my man. I wanted him to be welcome among my friends. He claimed he wasn't a people person, but I kept telling him he had to grow out of that because I am a people person. I love meeting new people. I asked him, "How are we going to be in a relationship and you don't like people and I like people?" He just said we would work it out. "I know we will," I said. As we walked to the car, Darius went to the driver's side. I could hear John in the background. *I know that bitch is not letting him drive my car.*

The ceremony was tiring. He asked, "Can we spend the night in Carvertown?" Carvertown was his home town. As we reached the city limits, he told me he wanted to check on his house. I said, "What house?" He said, "Mine." "Didn't you tell me you lived with your cousin?" I asked him, and he said, "Yes, this is the house that I used to live in." I didn't say anything because I felt it would not be same house as his ex-wife.

When we arrived, he asked me to come in. I said, "No, I am not going in that woman's house. I don't feel right." He said, "She has moved out. I need to make sure everything is secure." I proceeded to get out of the car and go into the house. When we walked in, it didn't look like she had moved a thing. He showed me around the place like we were at an open house. He showed me the hardwood floors that he had refurbished by hand. He was very proud.

As we walked from room to room, I observed Darius constantly putting his hands on me as if he was getting aroused. When we were in their bedroom, he put his hands on my waist to pull me close. I allowed him to do so. Then he tried to nudge me toward the bed, but I would not budge. I quickly turned and walked out of the room. I entered into the living room. He followed me, and I said, "I know you are not thinking what you, are thinking." He said, "I can't help it. You get me excited." "Well," I said, "you gonna have to wait until we get to the hotel." Darius looked at me and said, "I can't and I won't wait." He grabbed me and pushed me toward to sofa and slid his hands under my skirt and tore away my panties. He pressed his body hard against mine to keep me from moving. Then he unzipped his pants and pulled himself out. He penetrated me quickly. I was already moist. Because he was taking a risk, it was over soon.

After making love, we lay there on the sofa and he said that after the divorce he might gain the house. He asked what did I think about moving here. This would be a great place for him and I could live here. I said, "I don't want to live here. Can we leave? I feel sick."

We quickly got dressed and left. In the car, I said to him, "I can't believe we did that." He said, "Are you going to be OK?" I said, "No. I asked you, can you take me home?" He said, "You sure you want to go home? We can finish where we left off," but I said, "I want to go home." He turned the car around and took me home.

Chapter 13

Darius knew I wasn't happy with the incident that had happened the past weekend in his ex-wife's house. He kept leaving little special gifts and notes on my desk at work. Finally, when he discovered that I couldn't be bought, he asked could I spend the weekend with him in Savannah. He would arrange for us to have a room overlooking the ocean. We could watch the sun set and rise. We could leave Friday morning. He asked could I arrange for a baby sitter so we could spend the entire weekend together. I was hesitant. I knew I could get away for one night, but not two. My mom and Lessie would have a fit. But I wanted to go. I love the ocean, even though I can't swim. I just like looking at it, watching the sun rise and set. It is God's work.

So I asked him, since he was making all the plans, did he have babysitting money? He said yes, and I said, "Then I have a babysitter." I told him it would at least take a hundred dollars. Lessie loves cash. I figured if I gave her sixty dollars up front and then forty when we came back as a tip, she would be happy.

As I knew she would, Lessie said no. "The whole weekend? I love my grandkids," she said, "but, Jesus, two nights is too much." "Is that your final answer?" I asked. She said, "Just let me think about it." I reached in my pocket and laid the sixty dollars on the table along with a pack of cigarettes and said, "Will this help you with your thinking?" She looked and said, "As a matter of fact, I love my grandkids. We can spend the weekend together." I smiled and left her to gather up her reward.

As they say, money talks and bullshit walks.

Friday morning on the drive down to Savannah, we had light conversation. I was careful not to bring up that night at his house. I really didn't want to spoil my pampering, but on the way back it is on. Arriving in Savannah, we visited the Riverstreet and downtown. There is so much history here. It is so peaceful. The historic houses and old trees let you know you can live a long time if you take care of yourself. Darius acted as if he was the tour guide and summoned a horse and buggy to give us a ride. He said, "You are a queen. You needed to be treated as such."

After the ride, he wanted to stop in some of the taverns, but I am not much of a drinker. After a couple of shots of Irish rum, I was really feeling it. "Can we go?" I asked. He smiled and said, "Yes. We need to check in our room before four p.m. We're already running late."

Our ride to Tybee Island seemed like forever. I guess I was in a hurry to get there. Even though we had been together several times, somehow this was different, as if it might be the last time. Being a little shy, I wasn't outgoing in the sex department like Darius was. I wanted to express myself a little more. He was driving. I leaned over and began to rub him in his crotch. He looked surprised. I could feel his manhood harden up. My hand kept stroking him, up and down, and he moved in his seat and said, "Someone can't wait to get to the room." I didn't say anything. I stopped rubbing him and fondled with his zipper. I slowly unzipped his pants down and reached inside his shorts. He hit the brakes, as if he was trying to gain control. But it was not the car that he was trying to control. It was the lust and desire that I had awakened in his body.

As I pulled him out, I massaged him thoroughly just to tease him a little bit and let him know this was going to be a good weekend. I slowly bent down to take him in my mouth. But instead of taking him, I just kissed the top of it and placed it back in his pants.

Darius looked so confused. I knew he wanted me to continue, but he didn't ask because I had never acted this way before with him.

Once we checked into our room, he tore my clothes off. He could not get enough of me. After two hours, we lay in each other's body fluids.

Then he brought up the event that had happened in the car. He said, "I always wanted you to do that, but I knew you would do it in your own time." I turned and said, "And I am still not ready. Be patient." He said, "No problem. I will always have that image in mind. I can work with that." "I believe a man and woman should be married when they have oral sex," I told him, and he said, "You have never stop me when I do you." I said, "No. You don't give me a chance. Do you want me to stop?" I said, "I believe that is your decision. Believe me, I enjoy it, but I don't have to have it."

I noticed that the sun was going down on the west side of the island over the water, which is between the island and Savannah, and asked, "Can we sit on the balcony and watch the sun set?" "Why?" he said, and I said, "Why not? Don't you want to see the sun drop behind the ocean, the moonlight dancing across the water, and watch the sun sneak from behind the waves, trying to see if you are waiting for it to come up?" He said, "You made your point. Let's go. You are a real romantic." I said, "Yes. This is a special time in our life and we need to enjoy it." We spent the next two days walking and talking, sharing one another's thoughts and ideas. I wanted him to know, even though he was in my life, *please don't forget that I have kids.*

Chapter 14

I have always been known for getting my way. No matter how long it takes. After months of dating, I really wanted Darius to attend functions and gatherings with me. Whether it's a cookout or a high society party, no one wants to attend a function alone, especially when you are supposed to have a man of your own that could go with you. Deep down inside, I guess I wasn't satisfied with the way he was, being private and anti-social. I just wanted him to be a part of my world, but I could not, or would not, change the way my world was. I was happy and content with it, except for not having a man. If he really wanted me, he'd have to conform a little bit.

My cousin, Cordaisha, was going all out for her wedding. Her fiancé was having a bachelor party, and all of my peeps and their significant others, boyfriends, and spouses would be attending. Naturally, we would have a bachelorette party for Cordaisha to send her out with a bang.

I had to come up with a game plan to get Darius to go to the bachelor party. I should have been a coach for the NBA. I am always working on a game plan to win. Truthfully, back in the day, I played more games than the NBA. I had winning and losing seasons, but I always played to win. I figured if Darius hung out with the boys, it was a shoo-in that he would not have a problem with me hanging out with the girls.

See, the girls already had a stripper named Shy lined up. Let me just say this: *There was nothing shy about him.* The pictures I saw of him just made me just think was it like that in person. They say a picture can say a thousand words. Shy's picture said two words: Big D***. But since advanced technology has come into play, you can't always believe what pictures say. His penis may have been altered, or in Shy's case enhanced, if you know what I mean. But being nosy, I had to see—was the pictures live or was it Memorex?

I realize that if you are reading this, you wondering why I would want to see a d*** that didn't belong to me. You are being judgmental, but guess what? Stop before you have an aneurysm. If you have eyes, you can't tell me you haven't looked at someone that didn't belong to you. Better yet, sometime in your life you have imagined what someone was bringing to the table.

There is nothing wrong with window shopping from time to time. That is what my granddaddy told my grandmother. He said you can look at the items in window. Looking is free. It is when you go in the store, buy it, bring it home, and then try to return it to the store after you wear it that is the problem. In the end, you know you can't afford it, or it was not worth the time, money, and energy you put in it.

Everybody knows that. The stuff you see in the window is expensive. You end up buying shoes, earrings, and a pocketbook, and it is just like any other outfit. Once you wear it one time, it is not the same. It may even break you out and leave you with a rash.

Back to my plan to go to the bachelorette party. I got to get his ass to that bachelor party so I can hang with the girls. I don't want my friends to think I am on lockdown where I can't go out. Peer pressure is a bitch.

The plan is to go through all my friends' significant others and husbands to see who would have something in common with Darius. I have to find a guinea pig who I know will fall for my plan. A guinea pig to bait Darius. The guinea pig will be my best friend Maxine's husband, Sylvester. He is always easily persuaded to do things. I figure he just likes see if I'll get caught. He knew I was up no good. Sylvester and Darius had gone to the same alma mater. That was the common denominator.

So I called Maxine, told her my plan, and arranged a visit at their home when Sylvester would be there. Sylvester and Maxine had been together for twelve years and married for four of them. They had two kids. They were the ideal couple and had accomplished a lot together. They had built a home together and he supported her when she was in school. If she dropped the ball, he picked it up like married people should do. He didn't chase behind her, and she didn't chase behind him. They were both respectful and knew that no one was to come between them. Their marriage was not one of convenience; it was a marriage of two people together as one. Our friends and I only hoped that we could have what they have. Of course they had their problems, too. Who doesn't? They have survived a lot of storms.

Their home has always been the spot where we had events. New Year's parties. Birthday parties. Christmas and anniversary parties. They loved to party, and it was a huge house.

As I drove up to their home, I pulled out my best daytime actress mode. I had to fool Sylvester so I could go to this bachelorette party. I put on this concerned girlfriend act that I loved him, which I did. As Maxine let me in, I could see Sylvester smiling. He got up and gave me a hug and asked, "Where have you been?" I said, "Just chilling and working hard." He said, "You still look good. I guess you going to that party this Friday?" I said no. He said, "You are not going?" I said no again. Sylvester took a sip out of his glass and said, "Damn, I got to give it to Darius." I said, "No. I love him, so why should I go to see a man I can't take home with me? I have that at home."

Surprisingly, Sylvester said OK. Then he said, "Well, Max is going and I am going to the bachelor party. We will both get hot and bothered and come home and work it out." I said, "You know, I envy your relationship with Max. I wish Darius could see it that way." I told Sylvester that Darius wanted to go to the bachelor party, but he didn't think he would know anybody there. Sylvester jumped at the chance. He wanted to go without any incident from Maxine.

So Sylvester began his interrogation. "You want me to take your boyfriend to a bachelor party with strippers? And you are not going to get mad?" "No," I said, "because he is going to be with you, and you are married." I also said, "I know you are the most faithful husband that is still left. I just would feel safer if he was with you." Sylvester even said, "I guess you have a point. Besides, all the gang will be there."

"See?" I said. "You just don't know, I got to get Darius to fit in. If I don't, I will never get to see you and Maxine. Did you see me at your anniversary party? Did you see me at your birthday party?" Sylvester said, "No. By the way, where my gift is?" I said, "In the store." I told him Darius was trying to keep a sister on lockdown.

Sylvester said, "I understand. And if you are on lockdown, Maxine is going to be upset. Because all you gonna do is call my house late at night complaining about your situation, and she is going to take it out on me. So, yes, I will help out."

I gave him a hug and said thank you. Sylvester said, "Besides that, I need to see a little rump shaking, anyway." He saw Maxine give him that evil eye and changed his tune right away, adding, "I bet they will have strippers with a tiger butt. You know, the one with stretch marks. They are not going to be like my baby boom bottom, tight and firm." I said to Sylvester, "That is too much information!"

Maxine just got up and gave me a wink and I gave Sylvester Darius's number and told him that I would let Darius know he will be calling.

I gave my girl a hug as I was leaving and whispered, "Call you later." As I got in my car, I said thank you to the Lord and asked for forgiveness for lying.

Chapter 15

The bachelorette party was off the chain. Not only did we have one stripper, we had three. Sexual Chocolate. Liquid Sunshine. And Shy.

People used to say, *Be careful for what you ask for*. We got a lot at this party. Shy was about 5'10" and had smooth pecan tan skin. Sexual Chocolate looked like a bowl of Häagen Dazs ice cream. Liquid Sunshine let you know why light-skinned brothers were making a comeback. He had the prettiest long hair and hazel eyes. I could not help but ask why was his name Liquid Sunshine. I figured Sunshine because of his complexion, but what did Liquid have to do with it?

Then the promoter came on the stage and introduced him. "Liquid Sunshine means rain," he said. "Raise your hand if you are raining in your panties." Then he said, "Never mind. You all won't admit it if you were wet." We all laughed.

These strippers were good. They picked out all the women that could not handle them, the women at the party that were timid and quiet. I was waiting for one to dance up on me. I was going make him earn these five one dollar bills. (Y'all know I am cheap.) Shy would be named Outgoing. Sexual Chocolate should be renamed Iced Tea. And Liquid Sunshine? I'll rename him Dark Cloud. Back in the day, before I became committed, my girlfriends and I loved to party, but we had to adjust our life style when we had kids. We would have finished them and they would have a new name on their birth certificates. We always used protection. I kept this life a secret.

Darius had me on lockdown for a year. It is not that I didn't mind. I loved him. There was nothing I would not do for him. When I am in a relationship, I am not a cheater. I never want to experience the boomerang effect. The boomerang effect is if you do something wrong and know it, then it will come back to you. I had already started practicing *what is mine is yours and what is yours is mine.* I didn't have a problem letting him drive my car to the party. He belonged to me. I belonged to him.

I always like hanging out with my girls. If you don't have trust, what do you have? If anyone wanted to cheat, it only took ten minutes, if that long. You could meet up someplace, take off your clothes if you need to do that, and *do the do*. Clean up, if you have proper hygiene products, and put or arrange your clothes back on. Give a brief hug and kiss and say, "I'll call you later." Look around to make sure nobody saw you and get in your car and drive off like you were leaving to put out a fire. On a good day, it will be less than ten minutes. If the woman wears a dress or a skirt with no panties.

When I was in my younger days, these acts were a common practice. I used to help my friends cheat and sneak. But as you grow older, you live and learn that it is not worth it. No one wants to be labeled a whore. I did not want my kids to know that side of me. Yes, I gave it up. The relationships I have had maybe weren't the best, but I didn't cheat or run around.

The fear of getting caught always played in my mind. The fear of getting caught and looking like a Dalmatian. It was the fear of catching a disease that could take me away from my children. The fear of someone on the playground calling their mom bad names. I wasn't perfect, but, I had to be perfect in my kids' eyes.

One thing for sure that I have learned is you can't stop anybody from cheating if they want to. If there is a will, there is a way. The only person that can stop them is them. AIDS may have slowed people down, but not enough. Besides, cheating is an art form. Men and women make promises to each other behind their significant others, fiancés, lovers, and husband and wives back until they get in the bed or the back of a car together. They promise the sun and the moon. In the end, all they get is rain, tornadoes, thunderstorms, and hurricanes. Especially if and when they get caught in the act.

After the party, I was dead tired. I called Lessie to see if I could pick up the kids in the morning. She said yes and hung up. Then she called me back and asked me did I speak to Maxine. I said no. She said that Darius had had a wreck and had to be airlifted to the hospital. It was serious.

My world stopped. All I could think was, *It was my fault.* I had convinced him to go to the bachelor party when he really didn't want to go. Then I'd made it better for him by giving him my car.

I asked Lessie what hospital, but she didn't know, Maxine was gonna call later when she found out more information. I was in a daze. Lessie said, "Don't go down that road until she calls you and don't go by yourself." She actually sounded like a caring mother. I gained some respect for her that night.

Chapter 16

As I waited for Maxine to call, which took an eternity. When she finally called, she told me Darius's car had flipped twice and landed on him. He was thrown out because he didn't have his seat belt on. He was following Sylvester home, but when Stephen looked in the mirror, he didn't see his car lights. Stephen said it had been light raining, so he slowed down and waited, but still no car lights. He turned around and went back. He saw a truck stopped in the road and the driver said he'd seen a car go off the road.

Maxine said Sylvester and the driver saw the car tracks, but because it was so dark, they had to use the headlight of their vehicles to see. Sylvester said that they could see the car in the woods upside down, but they were afraid to go near because it might explode. The truck driver told Sylvester to stay there while he drove to town for help. He realized that Sylvester had been drinking. In the end, she said, Stephen had too much to drink and Darius had, too. I said, "Too much to drink? Darius don't drink that much."

She ended by saying, "Sylvester said that when the fire team and ambulance arrived, they searched for him. They heard him as they got near the car. He was pinned under the car and was alive."

I could not believe what she was saying. I was numb. How could this happen to Darius? What would his girls think? How I am going to tell his family? I didn't even know what hospital he was at. I asked Maxine to help me call the hospitals so I could call his family and let them know. But the hospitals we called would not release any information over the phone.

I sat there, thinking. What was our next move? All I could think of was, What would I do without him? The kids and him and I were so good together. Why does everything have to go wrong? I was so selfish, too busy trying to get what I wanted, not thinking about him. *This is my fault.*

The phone rang, startling me, and I almost hung up on the person on the other end. It was an orderly from the Emory University Hospital. The orderly said that Darius Howard had asked him to call me to let me know he was all right. "Don't come to the hospital, though," he said. "They are running tests." I wouldn't be able to see him yet. He also said Darius said he was sorry for wrecking my car. I smiled and told the orderly to tell him that's why the Lord let him live. So I could beat him up about my car. The orderly gave me his room number, phone number, and the visiting hours. I lay back on the sofa sighed a sigh of deep relief that he was all right. I thanked the Lord for not taking him from me yet.

Then I took a long bath so I could get some rest, because in the morning I would be going to the hospital to see my man.

Chapter 17

As I drove to the hospital, I felt good. I had talked to his mom, who was there already. She kept asking me when I was gonna arrive and how long was I staying. I told her I didn't have a clue. I let her know that my kids were at my mom, so I was no hurry to get back home. Lessie can be understanding as long as I don't wear out my welcome. Emory University Hospital in Atlanta isn't hard to find, not for me, anyway. I have relatives in and near Atlanta. I know my way around quite a bit. The problem with Atlanta is the parking. They try to pay for this city by making you pay to park in it.

When I go inside the hospital, the nurse takes out some time to show me where to go. She asks me what happened and I tell her. "Well," she says, "just have faith that he will be coming home to you soon." I smile at her as I get out of the elevator on his floor. "Thank you."

Darius's mother and aunt are outside the room in the hallway. They look worried. "Hello," I say. "Is everything all right?" They look at each other. His aunt speaks up. "Darius's wife is in the room with him." "OK," I say. "She brought the girls to visit. That is nothing." "No," Auntie says, "you don't understand. She is his next of kin. She has the power of attorney since he can't help himself." "What you mean, he can't help himself." His mom says, "He is paralyzed," and I fall to my knees and put my head in my hands and cry. "I thought he was fine. He had an orderly to call me and let me know he was sorry for the car". Auntie says, "He is going to be fine. Just that he may not walk again, and he will need someone to take care of him. She is his wife. They were not divorced. We don't like it, but there's nothing we can do."

I attempt to gain control; I don't want to call attention to myself. His mother says, "I will go inside to let him know you are here and find out will she let you see him." I say, "Let me see him, I been seeing him a whole year, and she was nowhere in the picture, and now she appears and everything changes." His mother says, "Yes. It is not her fault. Darius should have gotten a divorce. He do like most men, they leave their wives and they're too cheap to get a divorce. Calm down," she adds. "I know how you feel."

At this point, I don't know who to trust. I know how we are with some of my in-laws. No matter what our brothers did, we are still buddies with the wife, even after the divorce. They are blood to us. So when a new one comes along, we are hesitant to allow her in the family. We had one of my brothers' second wife call each one us and say, "I didn't marry you, I married him, and if you don't like me, I don't care." I wasn't mad at her because I understood. I can't do nothing for my brother. That's her job. But she struck a nerve with the family, and we let her know she didn't marry us. We treated her so cold until she left him. I felt sorry for her. My brother should have stood up for his feelings and hers, but his first wife was always around. It looked like we were all two faced. But we couldn't be friends with both. We had to decide to be a Confederate or a Yankee. We all were supposed to be grownup folks and set the example. Sometimes I wonder why we revert to childish ways.

As I wait for his mom to return, which seems like an eternity, I want to leave. I don't know this woman. She doesn't know me, either. Back in the day, I didn't mind beating a bitch's ass, so she better not step wrong. Besides I never have believed in fighting over a man. Not when you can find another one. I often wonder why anyone would fight over a man or woman. It is not worth it. If she only knew I was bluffing, because not only did Darius have me on lockdown, but my children and my job had me, too. There is no way I am going to jail and lose my job for beating a bitch's ass for her to end up with the man.

Women need to form alliances. When a man gets out of line, jump on his ass. No, you may not beat him, but ain't nothing wrong with trying to beat his ass. He'll know you are not one to play with. Why fight the other woman?

I make up my mind to leave, but his mother comes out and says that Courtney said I can come in. I cannot believe it. I got to answer to a woman I have never seen. As I enter the room, all I can see is tubes hooked up to Darius as he lies there. I can feel the tears roll down my face. He looks at me and says, "Don't cry, I am going to be alright. Just wait and see." I ask him, "Are you sure?" At this time, I hear someone coughing as I reach to hold his hand. I don't look up because Darius is staring in my eyes. But being a fighter from the street, my sixth sense feels her moving. I look up and she holds her hand out and introduces herself. "I am Courtney, Darius's wife and the mother of his kids." Now Darius had already told me that even though her first child was not his, he treated her as such. I say to Courtney, "I know, and your daughter is so respectful and has good manners. She gets along great with my kids. You did a good job." I know that is some introduction. See, you have to get in every word just in case you have to tongue wrestle and argue. I refuse to shake her hand. I know she is fronting that she is being sincere.

She gives me that look and says, "I wasn't aware you knew my daughter," but Darius interrupts and says, "Courtney, don't play dumb. You know that McKenzie and I have been seeing each other since we have been separated."

She says, "I must have forgotten you are the one he is seeing. I am so overwhelmed, you know, with your accident, and all." He asks her, could she leave us alone, and she smiles and says, "Are you going to tell her that you are coming home with me when you are released from the hospital?" Then she looks at me and says, "I can't wait to get him home and take care of him. It is going to be a pleasure."

He doesn't say anything. After she leaves, he asks for a hug and I give him a quick one. Then I ask, "Do I need to leave? This is so awkward. I can't embarrass myself about a man. I refuse to be the subject of people's conversation. Better, yet I know you don't want to deal with it, but call me when you want to see me. I will be calling to check on you. I love you, you mean everything to me, but I love you enough to walk away. It is me or her."

He says he understands. I lean down, give him a hug, and whisper that everything is going to be all right. I walk out of the room and observe the interaction between his family and her and announce that I am leaving. Courtney says, "Well, call me in advance and let me know when you are coming again. It was nice meeting you."

"The pleasure was all mine," I say. "It is always nice to meet the ex-wife."

As I walk toward the elevator, I can feel her eyes burning a hole in my back. I think, *Please don't mess with me today, your ass will be in a bed right beside him. It will not be a motor vehicle accident. It will be a mad black woman accident.*

The day is a bad day. My car is totaled, Darius is paralyzed, I have driven three hours, and his wife out of nowhere is running things. What else can happen?

Chapter 18

On the way home, I'm too upset to worry about Darius. How could I allow myself to stoop so low? I should have been concerned about his condition. This is messed up. He will not be able to walk again. I wonder, will I be able to continue our relationship if he has a disability? God knows, I love sex. Life without sex? Hmm, that will be a challenge. I need to stay optimistic. I say out loud, "He will walk again, I know he will." He was lying there like nothing was wrong with him, except the tubes. He didn't look paralyzed. I hope he'll call when that barracuda leaves and explain what is going on. I hate being in limbo.

Thank God, the day is Saturday and I don't have to deal with questions and comments about Darius's accident and marital situation at my job. I really don't have any answers for anybody except that he is in the hospital. Hell, this shit is just stupid as hell. How did I get in this one? How I am going to tell my family that Darius was fine? That his wife ran my ass out the hospital?

I arrive at Lessie's, "the PR representative," to pick up the kids and explain the situation. I don't tell her about the wife being at the hospital. She expresses how sorry she is for him and adds that the kids are at my house already. She asks about the car, but I tell her that I didn't have time to check on the car. I will do that Monday, and I did call the insurance company. She says they probably will not pay for it since he was driving, but I tell her that I have that kind of insurance that will pay. I'm glad that I have another car to drive. She says, "I thought you were going to stay in Atlanta tonight." I tell her that only immediate family can visit with him due to the floor he is on. She says, "Yeah, I thought about that when you left this morning."

Then she goes into that fussing mode. "How many times have I told you do not let anyone drive your car? Y'all just don't listen." She turns her back to me to walk to the stove and I ease out of my chair and creep out of the house. I don't feel like listening to church on Saturday. Besides, I know she got to get on her job and call everyone in the family about my car.

When I enter my house, the kids are eating pizza. They ask how Darius was doing and when is he coming home. The only thing I can say is, "He is fine. I need to lie down. Can you all be quiet for a while?"

I just wanted to lie down and wallow in my self-pity. How could I have been such a fool? I am so tired of these men with *hidden agendas*. They allow you to get trapped in with your feelings and then you can't let go. Once Darius gets well, he owes me a lot of explanation, but the main thing for now is him getting well without drama.

Lord, the man will not be able to walk. One of the guys from work would say this about older men: *If you are losing in your hips, you make it up with your lips.* I wonder, does that go for a man who is paralyzed?

I don't know if I can deal with someone being paralyzed. That is a big responsibility to take on. I have never been around someone with a disability. I don't know what to expect. Hell, I could not wait for my kids to get out of Pampers. I know I don't want to clean up after a grown man. As a matter of fact, Sean is leaving after graduation. One down, three to go. I can't wait for them to leave and I can be on my own. I love my children, I just want some *me time*. But I am told your children never go away. I say, they don't have to go away. Just get out, live on their own, and visit.

I hardly got any sleep that night. I tossed and turned. I finally gave up and watched TV. I dosed off at 6:30 a.m., only to be awakened by the phone. It was Darius asking me to come visit him. He said he had asked to Courtney to leave and not to come back unless she brought his daughter. He didn't go into detail. He just said he needed me. I told him I couldn't sleep at all that night because I was worried about him. I agreed to come back and see him after I got some sleep.

Chapter 19

I spent countless nights with him at Piedmont Hospital, where he was transferred for rehabilitation. Darius had been through extensive rehab so he could adapt to being home. I was able to take off a month, so I could visit with him. I had plenty of sick leave. My superintendent said that in his situation, Darius needed someone to stand by him, and he blessed me with the time off. Darius said that because I stood by him and he loved me so much, he wanted to make me an honest woman. I could not wait for him to tell me how he was going to make me an honest woman.

The hospital had taught him to be self-sufficient. He could drive a car with hand controls and dress and undress himself. Actually, he could do everything except walk. But when he said he wanted to go back to work, I was surprised. He was so optimistic that he would walk again. I tried to be optimistic, too, but I could not let him know how I really felt.

Once we were near the apartment he shared with his cousin, Darius said, "Let's put everything together and build a house. I want us to be a real family." I could not help but say, "You are not just saying that because you are paralyzed and you fear that you will not walk again?" He said no.

I said, "I will love you regardless whether you walk or not. I can't wait to live with you, either. It sounds like a great idea," I said. "Let's do it. I still own my land near my house. We could build there." But he said, "No. I do not want to live in your hometown or near your family. I do not want to live near my family, either. Let's find a location that is in between the two families." I said, "I really don't want my kids to change schools. They are settled here." He said, "We'll see." I was so happy.

Carlos and I stayed in an apartment when we were married, and now I really wanted the dream house for my kids. Front and back yards. We don't have to have a dog. Just a front and back yards so our kids can have somewhere to play safe. We agreed to put our finances together.

The next couple of days, I put my property up for sale and showed Darius the statements of my savings and checking account. I had to prove him that I was able to assist in the building our dream home.

Chapter 20

The next couple of months became trying for our relationship. We were getting used to not having real sex. He could not visit me because my house was not handicap accessible, and whenever I would visit him at his cousin's house, it was awkward because she was a full-fledged Christian. She must have known we were fooling around because she would play her gospel music very loud, no matter what time it was.

After making out in the car one night, I said to Darius, "I can't move forward with you unless you get a divorce. We do not need to have another incident like we had at the hospital. Hell, what if you had died? She probably wouldn't let me come to the funeral. What would that look like?" Darius said, "See, let me shut your mouth. I have already started divorce proceeding. We got to attend a three-day session to make sure we do not want to still be married. I promise I will get the divorce before we move in the house, so you can stop bugging me." He looked annoyed, especially when I suggested I could pay for it.

I said, "I am not bugging you, but what if the shoe was on the other foot? I know I could not be still married to someone else and living in a house with you. Or can I?" Darius said, "Look, I said I will get the divorce. She knows and you know you are the one I want. Didn't I prove to you in the hospital you are the one I want? Is that not good enough for you? What else do you want?"

I turned and looked at him and said, "D-I-V-O-R-C-E."

Chapter 21

After a whole week of going over floor plans for the house, where the lights would be placed, what kind of lights, what colors for the walls and windows, it was time for me to pamper myself by going to get a much needed hairdo. I had to visit my girl, Moria. Rich people pay therapists. Poor people get their therapy for free by going to the hair salon. Moria has always been one. No matter how much it may hurt you to hear it, she is going to tell you the truth and how she feels about it. She is not going to tell you what to do, but she will tell you the right thing. If you are close to her, she will keep you informed so you will not get hurt.

It wasn't a surprise when I called her and asked for appointment that she worked me in. She often says yes because we're best friends and should have been sisters. We have to keep one another up with our lives, whether good or bad. But this time, she added, "Because I need to make sure you are all right." "What did you hear?" I asked, and she said, "When you come for your therapy, I'll let you know." I knew there was no way she was going to tell me on the phone. She is one who loves to read your body language and facial expression. She wants to really know how you are feeling. I said, "Until tomorrow at two o'clock."

Besides that, I had a lot of other things on my mind. Darius would be returning to work in a wheelchair on Monday. It would be awkward, but I was happy because he could answer those nosy people's questions. No matter what I answered when someone asked about him, he wasn't pleased. He would say, "You talk too much. This person don't care. All they want to know is my business." He would get mad because I didn't give enough information, and I could not get it right. His progress was great, too great. It was as if he was not disabled. I often thought this myself. I kept hoping that he would walk again. I asked the Lord daily, "Do not take his ability to walk and to play with our children like a normal man."

But then, look at all the dead-beat dads that are walking around that don't spend any time with their children. They didn't know the value of quality time with children. If they did, they would know that the money that they pay is nothing in comparison with seeing their children smile when they are around. This is something I have never experienced because I don't have a father.

I often wonder what my life would be if I had my father around. He was just an image to me. My mother had a picture of him when he was younger, but what does he look like now? How is he, really? Just like any other kid, you want to know who brought you into the world, no matter how bad they may be. All I wanted was his approval. The one time I visited him in his hometown, he asked to borrow my car and stayed gone all night.

When I saw my sisters interact with their father, it was good but depressing. I often would check the mail as I was growing up to see if my dad had written to me. I would ask my grandmother if she knew anyone who would know him. She always responded, "Your grandfather is your daddy. He is the one taking care of you." Which was right. But it was not the same. And as history repeats itself, my children are going through the same thing. I know they will suffer, but I plan to make up the difference by trying to be both. That's why it is so important that I choose a family man that doesn't mind spending quality time with my kids. They need a strong male figure. I had found them one.

Once I sat in Moria's chair, I felt relaxed. But I felt she was holding back on our conversation. The crowd was light that day, mutual conversation for everyone. Then a coworker walked in. She spoke to everyone. She noticed me and walked over to where I was sitting and asking how was everything going. I said fine. She gave Moria an envelope and said thank you. I knew what that meant. She didn't have the money the day of her hair appointment. Moria is great about looking out for people. She knows she has a business to run, but if she can help you, she will. She often extends credit. She knows that we are all on a tight budget, just like she is. As my coworker made her exit, she tried to strike up a few conversations, like she was there on other business. But at one time another, we all have been in her shoes where we didn't have the money.

After my coworker walked out the door, Moria asked how the plans for the house were doing. I said fine. She said, "Are you sure?" I said, "Yes. What are you talking about?" She said, "That busy body, your coworker that just walked out of here, said that Darius is spreading the word around the prison that you are not moving in. This is his house. Did he come into some money?" I said no. *I* did. *I* sold the land *I* had and used to money *I* saved up toward building the house. She sighed and said she hoped everything would turn out all right. "I know you love money," she said. "If he knows you like I do, not only will he be paralyzed but he will be dead. I hope he does not mess over you about your money."

I started wondering, why was he spreading false rumors? He knows how our job thrives on drama. Moria begged me not say anything and to watch and see what happens. I agreed. She added, "Maybe your coworker is just jealous," and I said yeah. I knew she was trying to reassure me, but I knew she had more information. She was just waiting for the right time.

When she finished with me, I looked great and felt better. There is nothing like a visit to the salon to make a girl look good and feel good. I had been revitalized to battle Darius and any rumors.

Chapter 22

Monday morning, Darius was excited about going back to work. I asked myself, Why he couldn't be like most disabled people just stay home and draw a check? I also found myself not comfortable being in public with him. People stared at us as if they were thinking, What is she doing with him? She could have found someone that is walking. A lot of people were straightforward and asked me when they were able to get me alone, How is your sex life? Girl, what kind of sex can a man in a wheelchair give you besides oral sex?

They didn't know about medical advances. There is a way to have regular sex when you are paralyzed. They could implant an instrument to give the penis an erection. Or there was a device you could buy that can make a man have an erection. This is the one that they say a lot of older men buy.

But Darius was dead set against the implant. I asked him why. I told him what the doctors said, that the erections would last longer. Darius said, "What if I walk again? I don't want my business tampered with." So I left it alone. He said that he could and would satisfy me with the device. If it didn't work, then we would try other options, but not that. I gave up on the argument. After practice, the device worked fine. The only thing was there was no ejaculation. The doctor said Darius could not ejaculate, but he could, which was unusual.

When Darius arrived at work, he visited all of our coworkers as if he were a doctor making rounds. He did this as cordially as he could without causing a disturbance throughout the institution. I was hoping no one said I had said anything. He reassured them he was all right and thanked them for all they had done.

At the end of the day, I found him in his office getting ready to leave. I asked how his day was, and he said it was good. He looked as if he had something on his mind. He said, "I will go by the house to see what progress they are making." I said, "Good. Do you want me to follow you out?" He said, "No, I can handle it." Then he asked me to close the door to his office and have a seat. I did as instructed. He said, "I need you to do me a favor. I don't need you visiting the construction site. I will take care of the contractors." I asked him why, and he said, "Why do you want go?" I said, "Maybe because I have $8,000 invested and you don't."

He said, "All I am saying is let me as the man oversee the building of the house, and then you can take care of the decoration near its completion." I said, "I am just excited as you. I can't believe you are banning me." He said, "I will be taking pictures every week so you will know the progress. But for the last time, do not do not go near that house unless I tell you to." I sat there silently as he rolled to the door and opened it. He stopped in the doorway, and looked at me. "McKenzie," he said, "don't disobey me. It will not be good."

༺༻༺༻༺༻

Everything was going good for Darius at work. I hadn't visited the site, as he'd requested. It had been two weeks. Then an officer who lives down the street from the house stopped me at the grocery store. He said, "Girl that is a nice house you all building. From the framework looks like over 2,500 feet." I said thank you, and he asked how many bathrooms and bedroom. I said we hadn't decided yet. He said, "You must know. Once you decide on a floor plan, it is expensive to change it while building." I said, "Yeah, I know. Darius is handling it, and you know how you men are." He said, "Yeah, I understand. Let me know when and if I can help you all, since with his medical condition he will be limited." I said thank you and, "I will let him know what you said." I hated having to lie and pretend to people when the real truth was I didn't know a damn thang.

After the brother left, I was in complete confusion. I wanted to see the house. I decided I would wait until late in the evening after all the workers have left, and I would do a drive-by. Darius had a medical appointment in Augusta and he wouldn't be back until late. That is how

I knew he was lying about checking on the house.

It was getting close to sunset. I put on my jogging shoes, sweatpants, and a T-shirt and asked my uncle could I use his car to go to the store. I told him my car was acting like it was going to stall. He did not question me, but he knew I was up to something. He just said, "The same way you leave, the same way you need to bring it back." I said, "I got you."

As I was driving to the house, the sun was going down. I could not help but wonder what would happen if I got caught. But I didn't care. This was my house, just like it was his. My name was on the papers, too. As I got closer, I could tell no one was there. I stopped and parked on the opposite side of the road and looked in amazement at how much work they had done. It looked like a real house! They even had installed a window. I could not let well enough alone. I just had to get out of the car. As I got closer, I saw car lights. I prayed it was not him. The car kept going. I made it to the front door. It was unlocked. I thought to myself, I just need a quick walk through. I don't have to linger. Everything needs to be in order, just like he keeps saying. As I walked speedily through the house, I noticed cars were slowing down outside. Trying not be seen and not looking where I was going, I stepped on a nail. I hadn't put on my walking shoes with the thick soles. I'd been in such a hurry, I threw on my Keds.

I pulled my shoe off. That was a big mistake. I had blood running everywhere. I ran out to the car so I could find something for the wound. As I walked outside, a car pulled in. It was one of the officers from the third shift. I waved at her and she proceeded to get out of her car. I thought, I'll be damned. Just my luck. I positioned myself by my uncle's car so she couldn't see my foot. After the proper greeting, she told me she lived in the area and she wanted to welcome our family to the neighborhood. I said thank you and was wishing, Please don't tell anyone you saw me. I need to leave before the whole neighborhood showed up. After a quaint little chat, we went our ways.

I checked my uncle's trunk for something to wrap my foot in. I didn't want to get any blood on his carpet. I found an old towel that he used to wash his car. This would have to do. I sighed in relief and prayed that she wouldn't mention to Darius that she had seen me at the house.

Then I thought, Hell, I don't care! This is my house, too. I flew home so I could take care of my foot. I had to swap cars so I could go to the emergency room to get a tetanus shot. I guess that's what I get for going behind his back.

Chapter 23

The next week, I was on pins and needles. When Darius spoke about the house, I acted surprised. I noticed the things he mentioned had already been done to the house, but I just played the role, acting as if I had not seen the house. And then, just when I thought I was getting by, the control room officer radioed me and asked for my location. I told her I was at the M Building and she told me to stand by for a phone call. I was hoping it was not one of the kids and something was wrong. It was Darius. He sounded irate. In a vicious tone, he said, "Who in the hell told you to go to the house?" Before, I could answer and for the next five minutes, he wrote, read me, and published a sermon that would have made Oprah Book of the Month, except it was filled with so many *damns, shits,* and *asses,* and other curse words I don't care to mention. Since I was at work and could not properly respond, I just took it and smiled from time to time and said OK. I had an officer looking in my mouth. I knew Darius was finished when I heard the dial tone. Looking at the officer, I said in the phone, "Love you. Call you when I get home."

The officer looked at me and said, "I am so jealous of you and him. You both give me hope to one day have pure love." I said, "Yes, I truly have been blessed," but what I was thinking was, Yeah I just got *blessed* out and you just don't know how badly. As I walked out the building, I thought that damn lady didn't have to tell anyone she'd seen me.

I knew Darius was not finished with me. When I got home, I got the kids settled and waited for his next phone call. I was not planning on calling him so he could curse me out again. I figured he would call me again, so I just read a book and pouted.

It was bedtime, Darius still hadn't called. I turned over and went to sleep. The next morning I awakened to the alarm clock, hoping it was the telephone. At that point, I would have apologized to Darius for disobeying his rule, but still no phone call.

When I arrived at work, I met him in the hallway. He didn't even as much acknowledge that I was there, so I did the same. To me, it was not that serious. He needed to get over it. Besides that, I have somewhere to live and he needs my money.

By the end of the day, I had forgotten about the incident and him being upset at me. I clocked out and headed to my car. He was parked beside my car, waiting for me. I said to myself, "Oh, hell. Wheelchair is on the prowl." I had had a bad day and PMSing, and I knew this meeting wouldn't go like yesterday's phone call. When I walked to his side of his car, he motioned for me to go to the other side and get in. I did, when I was settled, he started talking. He started talking down to me, like he was scolding a child, but I cut him off before he got a good start. "Look," I said, "just forget it. I don't have time for your rules like I am an inmate. Keep your damn house. I don't need it."

I got out of his car and walked to mine. He was still talking. I gave him the hand, got in my car, and drove off. I have lived in the projects and in a single trailer. I am not materialistic, and that house does not define me. *I define that house.*

One trait Darius had not seen yet was if you back me in a corner, I am just like a cat. One way or another, I am coming out.

After a week of not talking, I received those famous roses he loves to send. He was asking forgiveness. I knew he would change his tune. He knew I was not begging him if I could help it. I had not done anything wrong. Then he called and asked did I want to see the house after work. He explained that they had made so much progress. I said yes and told him I would need to follow him because I had an errand to run. He asked what errand, but I said it was nothing worth mentioning. He said, "OK, let's meet in the parking lot at 4:30." I said, "No problem."

Now I knew that eventually I would have to choose between having what I want and having peace.

Chapter 24

Last week was the closing and the exchanging of money, and today I was doing my usual drive by the house. I saw the lights on in the house and Darius's car in the garage. It looked like he was unloading some items. Like a thief in the night, I drove further down the road and parked out of sight. I had spoken to him earlier that day and he had said he was going to bed early. Why did he lie to me? I walked toward the house. As I approached, I could see through the master bedroom window. Darius and his brother were discussing where to put his computer.

As I recalled, he'd said that the bank said we wouldn't be able to move in until the first of the month, which was another week and a half away. What in the hell was he doing here? And without me?

After his brother apparently carried the last items into the house, he left. I could see through the open blinds and watched Darius maneuver around the house. He went into the bedroom and made one last look, turned off the lights, and left the house. I hid behind the house until he left, then I felt for the key he had given me to go inside. I attempted to use the key to the door from the deck, but it would not work. I checked all the other doors with the key. The key was no good. It had worked when he gave it to me, but it didn't work now. Then I remembered that it opened the door inside the garage that allowed you to come into the house. That motherfucker, I thought. He knew I would come over here. Even if I did come, why would he keep someone out that has her name on the note, too? Better yet, someone who has agreed to pay over half the mortgage and all the bills in the house until you are financially able?

As I walked away, I was troubled. I had promised him I would not go to the house until the day of move-in. But then I asked myself, How do I approach him about putting his items in the house without causing an argument?

The next day, Darius called and asked did I want to go for a ride. I said yes and asked the Lord not to play my hand. As we were driving, I noticed we were heading toward the house. "Why are we going over there?" I asked, and he said, "There is something I need to show you." I played along with his little show.

When we arrived, he pressed the button on the remote control for the garage door. I asked him, did they leave an extra remote so I can have one for my car. "Yes," he said, "but there is not enough room for you to park. You will have to park outside. I need to keep the extra remote for emergency situations," he said. "You probably could park in the garage, but because I need space to put the wheelchair together, it will not be feasible. Also, you know, just in case this remote will not work, me being in the wheel chair and all, it will be difficult for me to get in." I said, "Well, let's see. Can we order one more remote for me? Being a female and it might be dark when I come home, I would like to have one. It might be dangerous at night." He sat there quietly, then responded, "I'll look into it." When I didn't say anything, he said, "We are not going to argue, are we?" I said, "No. I have all the answers I need."

Then he parked the car and said, "Wait here. I got a surprise for you." He got out of the car, put his wheelchair together, and went into the house. A few minutes later, he came to the door with no shirt on and said, "Welcome home." I got out the car and went inside. There were candles everywhere. All my doubts and fears went out the window. After a session of heated lovemaking, he held me and said, "I know this has been rough on you, but I wanted to do this my way. I have never had anything on my own. I just wanted to make sure everything went okay before we broadcast that we live here."

I said, "I just want you to remember this is *our* house, two people's, not one person's house. This is French language. We we we, not me me me." He laughed and said, "I got the picture." As I stood up and waited for him to get in his chair, I walked through the house and said, "I can't believe it this is our house." He said, "I know."

I remembered that he had been here last night, bringing in some things. I asked him, "Did you bring this stuff over here today?" He said, "Yes. I got off work early." I said, "Oh," and walked into the closet and looked at the clothes. Then I turned to him and said, "You were not moving in without me, were you?" He said, "No. Since I had some help with the setup, I decided to go ahead and bring some of my things." I said, "Good answer." He said, "Believe me, if I decide to do something, I will let you know." I said, "I hope." He said, "Now let's go back to bed for round two." I grinned and sat in his lap as we rolled toward the bed.

The rest is history.

Chapter 25

Just when I thought we were getting along good.... Well, everyone knows when a couple moves in a house together, nine times out of ten the female does what? The female always does all the decorating and the interior design for the home.

It was move-in day, and the kids and I were bringing in our stuff. Darius pulled me over to the side and said, "Look, I don't want anything on the walls." When I asked him why, he said it was because he "just didn't like pictures on the wall and it would leave holes." I looked at him and said, "If I put up a picture, it is because I am not going anywhere. I'll fix the holes. I understand your reservations about how people love to change their décor every two or three months, but that is not me. Once I finish hanging it there, I will leave it there for a couple of years." Darius said, "Look, no pictures on the wall." I said, "Are we are supposed to look at the plain walls? I don't think so. I get the feeling that you are telling me this is your house, not *our home*." Darius said, "I didn't say that. I just really would like the walls to stay like they are for now. Later we will hang up pictures. We need the thing to find the studs in the wall, so we can hang pictures." I said, "Well I'll pick up one from the hardware store on Monday." He gave me that look and rolled away in his wheelchair.

I thought to myself, *This is not adding up*. What is his problem? I always gave him the benefit of the doubt, but I would be decorating these walls, one way or another. Like a dog that pisses on a tree to mark his territory, I plan to hang those expensive pictures that I bought from Home Interior on these walls. First, I couldn't come see the house during construction. Second, he moved in before me. Now it's don't hang any damn pictures on the wall. Last, but not least, I put all my life savings in a house that I can't hang a picture in? He must be damn crazy.

No. I am the crazy one.

We had made a pact that we would never argue before the kids, so I gave up for the time being. When I went into the bedroom and closed the door, before I could say anything, he said, "When I get paid, I will pick up the stud finder and we will hang pictures together. But right now, give the kids something to do in their rooms, and I will be waiting in the bed naked." I did as I was told. It was late and the kids were tired, so I told them to get ready for bed. They had already eaten and Cameron had complained that he was sleepy. I told them we would finish unpacking tomorrow.

I had to remember what my great aunt said. In order to be a good wife to the man you love, you have to hold your tongue. Because he's the provider and the head of the household, you have to obey rules that you don't like. You have to fight to keep your husband, and all this starts when you are courting, not after you are married. I wish I could have asked her, was the man she married like Darius. This was my chance to be a wife again.

I knew this was my chance to have a complete family. We had our differences, but we loved each other. The nights I had watched him sleep in the hospital and be awakened by pain were so depressing, my heart went out to him. Sometimes, since it was my car, I wished it was me instead of him.

I knew he was hurting, but he smiled at me as if nothing was wrong. I never forget the day I thought he moved his leg and the doctors told him it was a false signal. The doctor explained that sometimes the nerves will send a signal to the brain, but because of the damage to his spine, it is stopped, so the nerve has a reaction, but it's a false movement.

He was so upset about that, he asked me to leave. During his hospital stay, he would not allow his kids or his ex-wife to visit. He knew he would walk again and did not want them to see him this way. Thank God, I went to a session with the counselor who helped me to prepare with his mood swings. She said, "This will be harder for you than him," and she also talked about depression and the hopes of walking again. She said Darius would experience a lot of symptoms and asked, would I be prepared if he doesn't walk again. I told her it doesn't matter if he walks or not, if you really love someone. Before we finished, she told me that he would need to come to Atlanta for therapy twice a month. She worked for a private physician group that could see their patients on the weekend if they had jobs. She also told me that Darius had signed up. I knew he was planning on going back to work, but I told her he hadn't mention therapy to me and I guessed he would be driving himself since they had taught him to drive. She said she didn't know how he would get there and added that he hadn't discussed the travel arrangements. I thanked her for the sessions and that they had prepared me for the worst.

I was glad he went to therapy, but I hated it that he could not make contact with me while he was there. He left on Saturday morning and came back on Sunday night. Twice a month, and he had to go religiously. When I asked, can I come along, he said there was nothing for me to do while he was there. He said I would be bored.

I'm a competitor. I had to be there for him, no matter what. I played to win. The real reason was not only did I love him, but I hoped if the shoe was on the other foot he would do the same for me. I vowed for better or worse, richer or poorer, sickness or health and to death do us part—I would stay with him. I became committed to see him through this. I would be his legs if he could not walk. He was my man.

I gave up on the fight for hanging up the pictures on the wall for the present. I just needed for us to have a smooth transition into our peaceful home.

Chapter 26

This morning I lie in my bed. I have been with Darius for three years. We have had good and bad times. Somehow, his only answer for my questions was sex and a rose. But I would not dare utter a word how bad it was with him. I blamed his changed behavior on the fact that he was paralyzed. But today I was going over the last few incidents at work and home. I thought we had made it through our first year. I decided that I was not happy at work anymore and needed a change. I needed to be able to advance. I needed the extra money, too. The house payments were high. Darius and I had agreed that because I didn't have any outstanding bills except a car payment, I would pay seventy percent of the mortgage and the utilities at the house for the first year when we moved in. He had a lot of credit cards that needed to be paid off, and he also had child support. He stated it would only take a year, then we could split 50/50 with the bills. Since we were a team and planned to be married, I supported him. I knew that after his divorce and the accident, he would have some financial setbacks, and I wanted to help him by doing what a wife (or soon-to-be wife) would do for her husband. I knew this arrangement would benefit our family.

My job situation was beginning to add more stress on my life than I needed. I had always been one that says, Don't stay with this job if it causes you misery. There are four types of supervisors: (1) by the book, and if you make a mistake, you are written up for it (2) coming on to you and trying to get you laid for favors, (3) prejudiced, and (4) fair and not biased. There were only a few fair supervisors, and someway or somehow they always leave. As the old saying goes, if you can't stand the heat get out of the kitchen. That was pretty much what a lot of my good supervisors and staff did. They left. My situation was a double deuce of two kinds of supervisors: those trying to get laid for favors and the prejudiced ones. It seems that no matter how hard you work, it is who you know not what you know that gets results.

But I had hope that the situation would get better. If it didn't, I would leave in search of something better. I looked at options every day. There was a female facility nearby that paid an extra five percent for their security level. They housed maximum security inmates that committed horrific crimes in our state.

I was also trying to handle coexisting in a new house with a man for a year and being a mom at the same time. This was partially my fault because I've been so independent for years. I made all the decisions in *my* house. Now I had to run everything by him. It was hard in the beginning, but now I had gotten used to it.

I remembered hearing a talk show host stating how it was impossible to work with your spouse. That became true with Darius and me. Darius was putting up this front that he is so insecure about fellow officers, especially male officers, socializing with me too much. He didn't like the way they looked at me or how they talked to me. I knew his new job as an investigator was boring because not much happens. That meant he had idle time to play with or, better yet, keep up with me.

Finally, I could not take him being jealous anymore. It was the last straw when I came home one day, and he looked at me and said, "Don't you need to get a larger uniform?" I said no, I haven't gained any weight. If anything, I've lost weight. He said, "Well your pants look too tight. You are working at a prison, not a tittie bar." "What are you talking about?" I asked him, and he said, "Do you know the other officers are talking about you acting like you want to get laid?" "That is talk with attitude," I said. "Show me concrete evidence and then approach me with that shit. By the way," I told him, "since we have been in this house together, that means we need to make arrangements to get hitched. I told you I am not shacking up over my kids. Maybe the officers wouldn't look at me that way if they knew I was hitched and not your house whore." I knew if I mentioned marriage it would put the end any argument he brought up.

This morning, I decided to put in for a transfer. I had previously discussed it with Darius, and he felt like it was a good idea, especially since it was more money. As a matter of fact, he was more than happy that I wanted to transfer. I made the phone call and was instructed what to do. It was simple First, fax the application and transfer form. Second, get my warden's approval.

I had the solution for my job situation. Now it was time to handle the relationship situation.

Chapter 27

I was always feeling guilty about living with him. I always do feel guilty. I had stopped ushering at my church because we were not right in the Lord's eyes. I remembered when he turned and looked at me and said "You love to bring up the Lord. Like you so righteous. Get over it. People live together for years." "That don't make it right," I said in a furious tone. "I am not planning on living with a man for years and then he ups and marries someone he didn't know for a year. I refuse to do that."

I mean, it does happen. We often see people staying married to each other until the kids are grown. Then, the year after the last child graduates, they separate and get a divorce. All those years of memories are thrown away to get a fresh new start with someone else.

What about the women who choose to live with a man for ten or fifteen years? Are these women not good enough to marry? Sometimes it is the woman who does not want to marry. They are crazy. You are sleeping, cooking, and living with him as if you are his wife. You might as well have the title. What if he comes home to you? A real man knows he has a good thing. He will respect you and marry you. I am talking about a real man.

After the children were in their own room, I announced to Darius that we have a mortgage together in our names for thirty years. "We need to have the same last name," I told him, "or I will leave." He said, "All because you want to be married. I told you, we will get married when the time is right." I said, "Maybe if I had a ring on my finger, those other officers wouldn't be making comments. I would know you are making a commitment." He said, "If you want to leave, fine with me." I said, "How are you gonna pay the bills?" He said, "Don't worry."

The kids came out to see what was going on, so I walked into our room and he followed me. I knew I had to make him understand that we need to finalize this. We are not a real family unless we are married. I am not going to be the cow that he can get free milk from, then, once I run out of milk, he moves to another cow. Or my milk is not good enough anymore. He is going to give me the respect I deserve. That is why I have lived alone for the last eight years. You may visit, but you will not live here with me until something better come along.

When John would spend the night, for example, he didn't even bring a change of clothes. I didn't want him to build up a wardrobe in my house. That cliché where a man hangs his hat is his home was not about happen in my house.

I knew he would follow me. I turned around and faced him. He said, "Look, you got to understand. It will happen." I said, "Well, I will move in the spare room until it happens," and with that I grabbed my pillow and a blanket from the bed and left the room. I said, "By the way, I have a job interview with another prison. I think I can advance quicker there as a female." He said, "If that what you want." I closed the door behind me. I was hoping he would follow me out the room and ask me to come back. But he didn't.

After searching through the attic, I found the old air mattress, the one we made love on the first night we stayed in the house and said, This will do fine until I move my bed. All through the night, I hoped he would come to my room and ask me to move back to our room. I hoped he would say we could go to the courthouse the next day. But it was only wishful thinking. When I got up to go to kitchen for a glass of water, I could see it was dark under the door, and I knew that if the TV was off, he was asleep. I just said to myself, What I have gotten myself into?

I return back to my flat air mattress of a bed and balled up in my usual fetal position. I drifted off and hoped for a better day in the morning.

Chapter 28

Morning went as usual. Darius had the nerve to get up and leave early so we would not interact. That was good. I gathered the kids up and went into our room, and Cameron asked, "What we are going to do in here?" I looked at him and said, "This is my bed." Cameron said, "And it is in your room." I said, "No, this is not my room anymore." After tugging and pulling, we disassembled the bed and moved it across the house to my new bedroom. I also took my TV. I replaced my bed in his room with the air mattress. Yes, the kids were late for school and I was late for work, but it was worth it. There is a time in a woman's life you have to put your foot down. I just wondered what his face would look like when he saw I had moved the bed. My interview was at four that afternoon, so I would not be able to see his surprised look.

When I arrived at work, he stopped me and asked how did I sleep. I said, "Good. How you doing?" and kept walking. I didn't give him a chance to respond.

When the kids and I got home, we could smell the aroma outside. I wondered, did he cook for us? We walk in and he spins around in the wheelchair and asks could he see me in the bedroom. I say, "OK, mine or yours?" He rolls past me into his room and I walk in behind him. I can't help but smile when I see that air bed. It's hard to maintain a serious look. I had to think of something fast to make me angry again because I knew he was pissed that I had disassembled the bed and moved my furniture out of the room. I remember how he had a hard time getting in his chair from the air mattress because the mattress is so low on the floor.

He turns around and asks me to close the door. I'm thinking he must be crazy. We have had arguments in the past, but nothing serious. We don't believe in violence. We just said what we had to say and left it alone. If we were angry, we just didn't say anything. Silence was the way we dealt with one another's shortcomings.

But here lately it seems as if he is comparing me to someone or trying to judge me for the way I am. I don't understand. I haven't changed. I am the same McKenzie.

He calls my name and says, "I asked you to close the door." "Sure," I say. I am feeling brave. I can handle what is coming. He calls me closer to him and says, "Have a seat." I look down at the air mattress on the floor. He says, "No. Have a seat in my lap." Like an obedient child, I obey him.

After I'm comfortable, he starts out, "I need to show you something." He opens up his drawer and pulls out a piece of paper. I noticed what looks like a ring box under a shirt in his drawer. He carefully unfolds the paper and says, "The divorce is final." I can't believe it. I don't know what to say. He then says, "I know I been a pain in the ass, but I love you and don't want to lose you. Guess what," he adds, "I don't have to attend therapy anymore." I say, "Wonderful. Now when can we split the bills 50/50?" But he says, "Not yet. Are you going to allow me to carry one of the kids as a dependent? You have always allowed me, and I'm just checking." I say, "Yes. Nothing has changed about that." He says, "Traveling back and forth has put a lot of strain on my pocketbook and I am still behind with my bills, But I am through traveling to therapy." "How long will it be?" I ask him. "I can't keep paying all the bills and buying groceries. You have to help." He says, "Maybe in a few months." I think for awhile and finally say, "I am still happy that the divorce is final."

I wait for the right moment to reach for the box while the drawer is open. I take the box out of the drawer. He looks at me in surprise and says, "How many times have I told you not to get something out of my drawer?" I say, "I know, but I couldn't help it." As I look at the gray velvet box, I ask if I can open it. He looks like he is not ready for me to open it, but then he says yes. I open the box. In it is the most gorgeous ring I have ever seen.

I'm speechless. I cannot breathe. Tears are rolling down my face. He says, "I was waiting for the right moment. I wanted to plan something special." He pats my back and says, "Did you hear me? Are you all right, McKenzie?" After getting my composure back, I say yes. The tears are flowing. It's the happiest moment of my life. We are engaged. I always believed in him. He was just taking too long.

Then I called the kids in and told them the news. We all did a group hug, and I asked, can we start making arrangements? He said we have plenty enough of time for that.

The next day I went to my job interview and landed the job. So I had two things to announce the following day: my transfer and my engagement.

My ring was huge, with diamonds everywhere. It had one large stone in the middle and twelve smaller stones around it. On each side, it had two rows of baguettes sparkling on the side. It was just perfect.

Chapter 29

The next two weeks went by fast. I could not wait to show off my ring. Everyone was happy for us. They couldn't wait for the wedding. But there was one problem: we had not set a date. Whenever I tried to bring up the date, Darius always had excuses.
I found out that I would be working on third shift at Oak Park State Prison. I knew this would be a challenge. These were females at Oak Park who have committed serious offenses and are in a maximum security prison. But I know my job and I love it. So it would be a challenge to break them in. I had to let them know I didn't put them in here and I can't let them out. I am here to provide a safe and secure environment. Anything else, they should have kept their asses home in order to have it.

This is my livelihood, and I can't let an inmate take it away from me. Once I entered the dorm on my first night, the inmates already knew I wasn't a new jack. They watched me and I watched them. Before lockdown, I had familiarized myself with majority of them by checking their photo IDs when they approached the desk.

Near lockdown time, it never fails—there is always an inmate that tries to be the thug. Yes, even female inmates have thugs. I announced to all the inmates that it was lockdown time and they had five minutes to report to their cells. This table with four inmates in the dayroom was playing cards as if they didn't hear me. Everyone else got up and went to their cells. I knew their fellow inmates were monitoring how I would handle the situations. I checked my watch, locked down the panel, and walked to the table and repeated, "You need to report to your cells." The inmates continued playing, except for one, who looked at me and said, "We need to finish this hand." I said, "You know what? You can finish your hand." I walked and made my rounds and closed all the cell doors. When I returned to the table, they said they were finished. I said,

"Really? I don't think so." The lead inmate said, "Why is that?" "Failure to follow is against the rules," I said, and she said, "You told us to finish our hand. I said, "I don't remember that, but what I do remember is that you are disrupting my count and you can receive a disciplinary report. But tonight I feel that we can work something out." They looked at each other and said, "Man, that is nasty." I said, "Yes, it is nasty, I mean the floor, that is, so if you would each get a broom and mop and detail the floor since you can't finish playing cards before lockdown." They didn't like it, but I knew I had them. I also had to let them know I am not the one to play with. When I asked them to do something, they needed to do it, not when they want to, but when I asked. After that night, everything was good. My dorm did as I instructed. They knew if I smelled smoke I would search their rooms because no smoking was allowed in the building. So they made sure they asked me for smoke breaks.

Once I came home, I knew it was going to peaceful and I could sleep all day. Darius would take the kids to school on his way to work and I would pick them up in the afternoon.

Chapter 30

I had been on my new job for six months and was finally taking some time off. I needed this time. I hardly saw Darius at all. He was working during the day and I was working at night. If we were both at home, I would be asleep and he had to go out for one reason or another. I was trying hard to change my shift to daytime. Darius had been complaining about taking the kids to school, and some mornings when I arrived home, Darius told me to take the kids to school. He knew I had been up all night, driven home, and was tired and sleepy, and he still wanted me to take them to school. He kept saying he was running late for work. I would not be mad at him if the school was not just down the road from his job.

I asked him about transferring back to his prison. That way, I could help out. He adamantly said, "No. They don't want you back out there." I said, "Who don't? Everyone is asking me to come back, even the supervisors." But he just said, "They are trying to make you feel good. They don't want you back out there," so I didn't bring it up again. I only added, "Well, you need to take the kids to school. I am not going to fall sleep on the highway, have a wreck, and die."

I was doing some cleaning when I heard the phone ring. I said, "Not today. I am not answering the phone." I had not heard from Chastity in a while, and when I heard her voice on my answer machine, I said, What in the hell do she want? She, of all people, she backstabbed me. She is the reason I am not a clerk anymore and had to become an officer. Well, I thought, I did track her down to brag about my engagement ring. Now I wondered what was so important that she needed to call me and want me to call her back. I erased her message without listening. The kids were spending the weekend with my grandmother, and Darius had left a note saying he would not be home until late. I had a hair appointment, but it was canceled. Today was my day to enjoy myself.

So I was home, taking in some quiet time. I thought maybe Darius and I could spend some alone time together, and I started planning a surprise for him for tonight. I checked the fridge. I didn't want to cook. I thought, I'll just call the Applebee's. They have great curbside service and steak dinners to go. Darius loves their steaks. I prepared the table, took a hot bath, put on a nice dress.

I had good news—I received a rebate for $5,500 for back taxes owed to me. I wanted to use it to plan a special trip for us and catch up some bills.

I drove to the restaurant with these happy thoughts and walked in and stood at the counter. The place was getting crowded. Then I heard this voice. I knew I had heard it before, it sounded so familiar. It was the counselor from the hospital. She was on her cell phone. I hoped she would finish her call before I left. I wanted to say hello.

After I paid for my dinners, I walked over to her table. She was finished with her call. She remembered me and asked what was I doing now and maybe we could get together. She said she was living in the area now. She was surprised to hear that Darius and I were still together. She even more surprised when I told her we were living together. It was great, catching up with her. I just had to tell her about the house and the ring. I had always felt from our last conversation that she doubted we would stay together. She sat there quietly as I went on and on, and when I finished, she said, "I knew Darius loved you, but I didn't have any idea this much." I explained to her about the dinner I was planning and I had to leave. She said she was waiting on a date. I told her have a nice dinner, gave her a hug, and left.

The time had flown by. I had to hurry home and get ready. I had a sexy outfit for Darius, but I only had an hour and half left to get everything ready. I checked the voice mails. Chastity had left her cell and home phone numbers and stated, "Please call."

I had finished everything. I was dressed and ready. To keep the dinner warm, I had placed it in the oven. I poured a drink and lay down on the sofa to watch TV.

Apparently, I dozed off. I awakened to the sound of Darius coming in the house. I looked at the clock. It was after midnight! He went into his room and closed the door, ignoring the fact that I was standing there wearing a sexy outfit.

I opened the door and asked what was wrong. He didn't look at me. He said, "Nothing I can't fix," and I said, "I miss you." He said, "Why? You saw me this morning." I said, "I planned a romantic evening for us," but he said, "I told you I was coming home late." "I know," I said. "I just wanted to surprise you." He looked up at me like he was disgusted and said, "I'm tired. Let's finish this in the morning." I said OK and turned around to clean up and put the dinner away.

He said, "McKenzie, we need to move your bed back in the other room." When I asked why, he said he was getting a new bed the doctor said he needed. "We can't afford that," I said, but he said, "I'll pay for it." "How?" I asked him. He said, "I have some money saved back." I said, "Well, if that is the case, when can we split the bills evenly?" He looked at me and turned to go to the bathroom without answering. I said, "OK, I can't wait to test it out. The kids and I will take care of it. What time we need to move the bed?" He said, "The bed will be here tomorrow," and I said, "OK, I'll pick them up and bring them home for the day. Can we have a movie night tomorrow?" He said, "We'll see."

I got into bed slowly not to awaken him. He slept on the other side, as if he was trying not to touch me. I knew something was wrong. I guessed it was another one of his mood swings he was going through, but then I saw his leg move, as if it wasn't happy with its position. I hadn't tested his legs in a long time. I reached over and pinched his thigh to see if he could feel it. Darius jumped up and asked, "What are you doing?"

I said, "Your leg moved." He said, "No, it didn't. I moved because I saw you moving." I said forget it and he said good night and silence filled the room. Here we were, two people lying in the same bed and not saying a word, just thinking.

I had to admit it. I knew something was wrong. I always knew something was wrong, but I could not see past it because I was trying to fulfill my dreams and goals. How long would it be before I know what it was? I knew he needed me. He couldn't afford to live here by himself. I was the one basically paying all the bills. I was secure in knowing that

I was not going anywhere. I decided I'd keep my rebate a secret. He was acting like an asshole.

Chapter 31

Next morning, he awakened me to go and get the kids. I called my grandmother and asked her to get them ready. She asked what was wrong, but I told her, "Nothing, I need them to help me with something in the house," and I would bring them back when we got through. She said all right, but she sounded as if she didn't believe me. I knew I should have told her right then and there about how Darius didn't want them or me to let other kids spend the night at house. I should also have told her about the toys incident. When we first moved in, if the kids left toys on the floor, Darius would roll through the house and pick them up and put them in a basket. Then, just to teach them a lesson, he would put the toys in the trash. But I had paid too much for those toys. I went behind him and took the toys back out of the trash. I just made the kids clean them up.

This morning, I asked him did he want any breakfast. He said no. "Look," he said, "I am not trying to rush you, but the people will be here in an hour or so." I said, "OK, I am going."

When the kids and I arrived back at the house, Darius had disassembled the bed and moved it himself. "What you need the kids for?" I asked him. I knew he had upper body strength, but this was serious. He said, "Once I got it loose, it wasn't hard." I said I was gone only forty-five minutes, and he said, "Yeah, but the delivery truck will be here soon. You can take the kids back." He gave each of the kids a hug and five dollars to spend for the weekend. They ran back to the car and waited for me.

As I drove away, Cameron said, "Mom, how did Darius move the bed?" I said I didn't know, but he said, "Yes, you do," and I said, "Cameron, what did I say?" He said, "I know what you said, but what are you thinking about?" I looked at Cameron, and he said, "I get the point. You don't want to talk about it."

Cameron was always the one who figured out stuff very fast. He didn't mind asking me what was wrong. He had to know. He wanted to be my protector. He loved Darius. Darius replaced his real father. I guess that was another reason I stayed with Darius. I knew it would hurt Cameron if anything happened with Darius and me. He played on Cameron all the time. Josh and Kira didn't act as if it bothered them, but they knew whatever Darius gave Cameron. Cameron would share with them. That is what kind of big brother he is.

On the drive to take the kids back to my grandmother, I had decided I was not going to spend the day at that house with him. I kept the rebate a secret and decided I would spend the day with one of my friends.

Chapter 32

On the drive back, I could hardly focus on how he moved that bed, and once I dropped the kids off, I decided to go see Maxine. Maxine told me about one of her cousins that had left her husband. She said her cousin left furniture, clothes, personal effects, and a two story house that was paid for. I said, "I am not leaving! I'll move to the other end of the house, but I am not leaving." Maxine said, "McKenzie, material things are not worth it if you can't sleep in them in peace. Remember John?"

"All the things he gave you," she said, "and he said he loved you. But I remember how he also gave you hell. But I had to give it to you. I remember how you packed up the car, put the VCR, the TV, all those clothes that he bought you, the children's toys that he bought over the years, and you drove it all to his momma's house and left it. You said you didn't want anything from him."

I said, "I remember." But I didn't want to be reminded about John. I said, "At least I didn't burn them up," and Maxine said, "The same with my cousin, and she wanted peace. He didn't allow her to work and she had to ask permission to leave the house. He had to know her schedule. Nobody apparently told him that they freed the slaves a hundred and fifty years ago. We would visit her in that big house," she said, "and they put up that front like they were all happy. But he treated her like shit behind those walls for years. On hot and cold days, he would not let her turn the air or heat on until he got home. The only time he allowed her was when the kids were home. You remember the wedding, don't you?" she asked. I nodded. She said, "That nigger stood up in the church crying before everyone like he was so in love. When they arrived in Hawaii on the honeymoon, he would not let her out the room do any sightseeing. He went sightseeing." I asked her, "How you know that?" She said she called her maid of honor, Tiffany, who was her best friend and can't keep a secret. She had my cousin on the speaker phone with some more of their friends. The problem was, the maid of honor didn't know my cousin was upset about the trip. The maid of honor called my aunt and, you know, the rest was history.

"A big house is nothing," Maxine said, "if two people don't agree. You want to be married and Darius don't. You pay the bills and Darius don't."

I said, "You know what? That reminds me. A couple weeks ago, the bank left a message about the payments being behind." She asked, "Did you say anything to Darius?" I said no. "I give him the money, and he pays all the bills. I don't worry about that." She said, "Girl, you better wake up!" I said, "I just don't deal with it. If it is behind, he'll need to catch it up. He is the one who manages the money." She said, "But I know you don't want your kids living in the dark, either."

I looked at the clock and got up. "Look," I said, "I got to go home. But I'll call you so we can do lunch and do our Christmas shopping," and she said, "Take care." She called to me and said, "When someone wants to go, let them go, and they'll come back." I smiled as I got in my car and drove away.

I knew Maxine was right. Cameron had it figured out, too. They say everything comes in threes. What is the third? I knew what the third was. I already knew Darius and I were not going to work out.

Chapter 33

I arrived home to find that the new furniture was in the bedroom and Darius was gone. He had left a note on the refrigerator: "Don't bother anything in the room." I thought, I am so tired of those damn famous notes.

I took this note as Don't put any of my clothes in the drawers. I walked into the garage to see if it needed sweeping and pressed the button on the wall that ran the garage door. The garage door hesitated as if it would not open. I tried it again. This time it opened. I wondered if I unplugged the door what would Darius do. After I swept the garage, I closed the garage door, then I took a ladder and climbed up to unplug the garage door. I almost fell when I heard a car drive by. I thought it was Darius.

Then I drove back to Maxine and left my car at her house. On the way back in her car, I told her what I suspected. When we arrived, I was happy to see that Darius was not home yet. She rushed me out of the car and said, "Call me later." I ran into the house and waited for Darius to come home.

I turned off all the lights so it would look like no one was home. Eventually, I heard Darius drive in. I watched him from the bedroom window. He loved to back the car into the garage. Finally, after a few minutes, he opened the car door. He put the wheelchair outside the car as he usually did and put it together. I said, "Damn, he can't walk." I started to walk away from the window, but then I heard footsteps. I said to myself, Is someone with him? I looked back out the window, and there he was. He was standing at the door and unlocking it. He walked in. I could see his shadow from the reflection of the outside light. He turned the garage light on. I could hear him unfolding the ladder. I waited a few minutes. When I heard the garage door open, I walked to the back door and knocked on the window.

He turned and looked at me through the door. It was like he had seen a ghost. I opened the door and walked into the garage. "Ain't this a bitch," I said. "You can walk." As I turned to walk into the house again, he grabbed my arm and said, "Let me explain." I snatched my arm away from him, went to my room on the other end of the house, and locked the door. Thank God, I can sleep in my bed and watch my own TV.

I should have been happy for him. I wanted to take a car and run over his ass again.

Chapter 34

Darius knocked at my door and called my name off and on during the night, but I didn't respond. I finally heard him say, "Have it your way." I turned the TV up louder and asked myself, What do I do now? Do I leave? Do I stay? He has been lying, but for how long? I gave up trying to figure it out and went to sleep.

I must have been dead tired. When I finally woke up and looked at the clock, it was two in the afternoon. I dragged my body out of bed and walked to the kids' bathroom and looked in the mirror. I looked terrible. I had bags under my eyes. Thank God, I was on vacation for the next week.

When I came out of the bathroom, he was standing there. He said, "There is a lot you don't understand." I said, "If there is, I don't want to know about it. All I ask is today I don't want to talk about it. I need to be alone to figure this out." He asked, "Can I please explain?" and I asked, "How long have you been walking?" He said, "A little while. I gradually got my feeling back." I asked, "Why don't I believe you?" He said, "This is my story and I am sticking to it whether you believe it or not."

When I didn't laugh, he said, "Please sit down so we can talk." Tears were rolling down my face. "I can't," I said, and I ran to my room and closed the door. I didn't hear him follow me. I only heard the sounds of the door and his car switching on to leave.

I stayed in my room in my misery all day and all night.

The next morning came too fast. I've always hated Monday mornings. Monday means going back to work. Thank God, my grandmother had agreed to keep the kids and let them catch the bus from her house.

I didn't hear Darius come in at all or leave for work. Since my TV was off, all I could hear was some damn woodpecker tapping. I tried to go back to sleep, but that woodpecker wouldn't let me. It seemed to be right outside my window. So I gave up on sleep and walked to the kitchen. When I got there, I turned around and looked out through the kitchen window. I saw some white person standing on the deck. It was a woman. She must have heard me. She turned around and came to the door. It was Chastity! I opened the door and asked, "What are you doing here?"

She said, "McKenzie, please do not curse me out like you did the last time. I know I backstabbed you and almost cost you your job. But please let me explain why I am here."

Chastity was the reason I became a correctional officer while I was out with Darius. The company didn't want to keep but one clerk, but she told them that I was never at work. She did all the work and ran the office. When I returned, they offered me one option—to become an officer or be terminated. I could not believe she did that to me. I was the one that trained her. I wouldn't speak to her, no matter what. The only time I did was when Darius gave me the ring and I announced our engagement before I transferred from the prison.

Chapter 35

But now, after listening to her pleading, I asked her, "Why are you here?" She said, "Well, I know you don't want to hear this from me, but Darius has been cheating on you with this counselor." I said, "Chastity, I can't take hearing any more bad news now," and she said, "Yes, you can and you will." She said, "Darius has been running around and making you look like a fool since you transferred. This bitch he met doing his therapy transferred to the prison as a counselor. I just found out that she has moved here and is living in a suburb in a nice house. Which by the way they are planning to share next month. See," Chastity said, "he told somebody who told me that he needed a woman with no kids and a bigger salary."

I just stared at her blankly. She then said, "But by the way you look, you already know. I have been calling you all weekend trying to tell you. He was planning to move you out of the house, but somehow he couldn't do it. So he stopped paying the bills. Girl, they are getting ready to foreclose on your house and you don't know it."

"Darius would not do that," I told her, but she said, "Yes, he would. Next week this house will be auctioned at the courthouse square." She looked around. "You must not know because you have not packed up anything." I said, "I am not going anywhere." She said, "Well, maybe I got it wrong, but your house is in the papers to be auctioned off next week." "You have to be wrong," I told her. "My job deposits my check into Darius' account each pay period so he can pay the note."

She said, "He ain't paying it."

Then she said, "One last thing. That ring was not meant for you. He told somebody you pulled it out of his drawer while you and him were talking. He didn't know how to take it back. He said he was trying to explain it to you, but you broke down and went to crying and said Yes, I will marry you. He said he didn't even ask you. And I am giving you the clean version of what he said."

"What is the name of the counselor?" I asked her. She said, "Teresa McCluskey," and I looked at her and said, "You got to be kidding. I know her. She worked at the hospital." Chastity said, "That's what I said! She been fucking your man since day one. Do you need my help in killing him? Because I know someone can arrange for the house to burn down with him in it."

I looked at her and said, "That sounds strange, coming from you, especially since you backstabbed me." She said, "Yes, I did, and I have had bad luck ever since, believe me. After you left, they cut my pay because they could not afford the salary I had. Hell, I should have become the officer! I fucked myself. There you have it," she said. "I was wrong, McKenzie. I have waited so long to tell you that. You were my friend. But Darius? I'm gonna curse his ass out."

I said, "No. Let it be. Let me handle it for now." Before she left, she said, "Don't tell nobody I came out here. I lied about not coming to work today. I had to come when he was not here." I told her I understood. "McKenzie," she said, "let me kill him. You have children. I don't want you to do something that you may lose them. You know this a redneck town. I am white. I will probably get off quicker than you."

I could not get mad at her saying that. She was right.

After she left, I made my plans to talk to Darius when and if he came back. I needed for him to tell me in my face.

Chapter 36

As soon as Darius walked in, I said, "We need to talk. I know we been through a lot, but the pain is killing me, and I really don't want to lose you or what we have. All I ask that we work this out. Let's do this right to please God and for the kids and for us. I will catch up the house payment. We can plan a date to go to the courthouse and get married. We can start over again from scratch. Let's put everything behind us," I pleaded with him, without breaking down.

He just sat there quietly, not even acknowledging me. I asked him, "Isn't what we have worth giving it another chance? Look at what we have been through. Doesn't it count for anything?"

Finally, he said, "You knew you had the money. Why were you hiding the fact? Besides, I am not ready to get married. I told you that already. You just don't get it. All we went through? This wasn't about us. This is about me. When you found out that I was seeing her, why you didn't move out with your money and start over?"

I was confused. "This is my home," I said, "and I didn't know about her. You don't love her. How could you? The many nights I sat at your bedside in the hospital and prayed for you to get better. I cleaned you up when you had accidents like you were a baby; I supported you and stood behind you. Now that you are able and walking again, you are leaving me for her? I can't believe you!" I shouted at him.

"You need to believe it," he said. "Since you won't leave, I'll leave. We don't have to shack up or live together. But you will not live in this house with another nigger. I will put your life on it. I plan to file bankruptcy. This way I won't have to be responsible for the house. The bank said the house will be foreclosed on Tuesday. They will sell it and you have to move. The deadline to purchase the house was up. The electricity will be turned off on Monday before the foreclosure." He said all of this like a villain with a master plan.

I asked when all that happened. I didn't remember receiving any mail.

I did not receive any mail.

He said, "I know you didn't receive any mail. I changed the address to the account." "You mean," I said, "there is no way to buy the house from you or the bank?" He said, "You got it. You need to move out before they set you out. I will be here on Saturday to move my things. Since you can't shack up and you are so full of God, you should be married to God."

"Ms. McCluskey will be a better wife," Darius said. "She got money. I baited her in just like I baited you. The limo and that cherry stem work every time. Don't get me wrong. I will miss the kids, especially Cameron, but I got to move on to bigger and better things. I am not planning on struggling all my life." Then he laughed.

When Darius opened the bedroom door, Ms. McCluskey walked out. She said, "No, Darius, you lose. The bigger and better things just move on." She walked past him and out the door. He followed her, but he could not stop her. As she drove away, I could hear Darius screaming at her. Then I heard Darius's car leaving.

Chapter 37

He moved out on Saturday and took all his belonging. He even took the damn refrigerator that I bought.

The week of the foreclosure, I tried again to convince Darius to file bankruptcy on the house. I told him with my credit I could buy the house from the bank, but he had to sign a form to come off the note. He refused. I gave up and figured that was him. I guess he wanted his credit messed up since he had all those bills. He said, "No. My lawyer said it would not be in my best interest." I said, "The kids and I will be homeless." Darius shouted at me, "You will make a way."

With tears in my eyes, I said, "If you don't want the house and say you can't afford it, do the Christian thing. Let me and kids have it. I can afford it. Just sign the papers at the bank so your name will not be on it."

Darius said, "You must think I'm crazy. No man will ever sleep in the house I built. If I can't have it, you can't either. And I am not a Christian."

I said, "You didn't build this house. We did."

He said, "When are you going to get off this bus? You can't be that stupid. If my money would have come through, I would have bought you out anyway. This house was for me and my girls. Not you. Did you believe we would have been the Brady Bunch? Yes, the sex was good, but I say again, No, I didn't want to marry you. You should remember one thing as long as you live. There are some women you date and some women you marry. Ask yourself, which one are you, after all this?" He stopped and said, "Before I leave, I need my ring back." I pulled it off and threw it at him. He picked it up and left.

When I arrived at the altar, the usher led me to a chair. My cousin came and stood behind me. Reverend Sherman asked me why I had come. I said for prayer and I want to rededicate myself to the Lord because I had lived in sin. There-I said it. The usher looked at me as if what kind of sin. Reverend Sherman said that was all he needed to know. He prayed with me and told me if I need counseling to give his missionary department for young women a call.

    I felt good. A weight had been lifted off of my shoulders. I was able to admit it out loud.

Epilogue
PART V

Chocolate Prince

Kevin called again last night. He must know by now that I am not interested. I refuse to date again. Once a month for the first two years, he called me like clockwork. Now, after six years, he just calls at Christmas, New Year's Day, and my birthday. I plan to wait for the kids to all be out of the house. I do not want to put them through any more emotional drama. After Darius, Cameron had counseling. Kira still asked about Michael and John. I have had four strikes in the last twenty years. Mona told me I was doing good. She says, "In this day and time, how many can name all of their sleeping partners?"

I am in my mid-forties. I just want to go to church, go to work, and be a mother. I don't need a man. I can pay all my bills, and sex is overrated. I had tried every approach in the dating game, and the only one left is to become a lesbian, but Darius did enough licking to last me a life time when he was paralyzed, so I knew being a lesbian is not about to happen. The main reason God destroyed Sodom and Gomorrah was because the men in the city tried to lay up with those angels He sent down. I also love what a man brings to the table, but that is what has gotten me in trouble all the years. But to each his own.

Right now, on this day in time, I am not wasting my time dating someone's son. I was married for nine years. I dated John for five years, Darius for five years, Michael for two years.

ACKNOWLEDGMENTS

I could not have done this without the Lord, Jesus Christ, the Father, The Son and the Holy Ghost. You all are first in my life, YES I AM YOUR CHILD.

I would like to show appreciation to the following churches that have given me spiritual guidance; Pine Grove AME Church, Donovan Ga.; Buckeye Baptist Church, East Dublin, Ga.; Williams Chapel Baptist Church, Dublin Ga.; Tarvers Grove Baptist Church, Bartow, GA.; Mt. Patmos Full Faith Gospel Church, Candler Rd. Decatur, GA.

To; Ashley, Brian, Janique and Janiah: let this be another lesson to learn. No matter what, don't let fears, rejection, denial, what someone may think of you and/or even say about you stop you. I know now only you can stop yourself. Nite Nite I love you; to my grandmother, Melzie Williams, My Aunts and Uncles Susie, and Jennette -Jimmie (Uncle Money), Aunt Yvonne and Uncle Ray Fann, Jasper and Carol Williams, Mahaila and Bobby Devero thank you for being there through all the hard times To; my mother Jant, sister; Tiff, and brother; Chad you really mean a lot to me; Ms. Deanna Cooley and Mike Bright (PurePote'ntial)-thank you being patient with me over the last two years and encouraging me to finish; Harlie Fulford Library, Wrightsville, GA., and Laurens Co. Memorial Library, Dublin, GA.- Thank you for allowing me to use your facilities; Keith "Preacher" Brown-Thanks for saying "just because you come from a small town-don't mean you have to have a small town mentality"; All my best friends , Priscilla Brown, Robin Horne, Crystal Baker, Gwen Ammons (I missed you), Cynthia C.J. Johnson, Hazel Stephen, Latasha Harrell, Jane Baker, Tracey Lemon, Tywanna Wright-Scott (my ace), Tammy Newton, Tracey Atkins, Tracey Poole, Letiticia Martin, James Blair, Constance Johnson (guardian angel), Courtney Thomas, Mathol Jordan, Reginald Fordham, Jerome Andrews, Anita Hall, Carolyn

Liggins and Sylvester Burton -

Special Thanks to my uncle Kenneth Williams and your wife Jeri for the encouragements

Last but not least, I have to give love to my dream team that make me look good, My Savior, Jesus Christ; My editor, Barbara Ardinger www.barbaraardinger.com, cover design Keith Saunders www.mariondesigns.com; web design Markerting Xtraordinaire III by Grego/grego@mx3g.net. If you don't have a church family-get one, because my church family is the greatest. Buckeye Baptist Church with Rev. Tracey Wheeler; where everyone is somebody. Without them and the Lord I would be lost. The last year I had to fight off negative comments, lies, and pure evilness from certain people and even some family members when I step out on faith to pursue my dream. But my church family and God stood by me and I made it through. I had to learn that evilness can mean for your good.

ABOUT THE AUTHOR

She is the mother of 3 children: Ashley, Anthony (Brian), and Janique (NeNe). She is a graduate of Johnson County High School of Wrightsville GA. and Heart of Georgia Technical College of Dublin, GA. She was a member of Phi Beta Lambda. She was born, raised in and resides in Wrightsville, GA. She is affiliated with Pine Grove AME Church in Donovan, GA.

Mail Order Form

Can't Let Go Part Two: The Hidden Agenda (18.95)

Shipping & Handling ($5.00)

Name:_____

Address:_____

City_____ State_____ Zip code:_____

Send checks or money orders to:

C C Fann
JABS Publications LLC
P O Box 81
Wrightsville, GA 31096

478-278-7956

Please allow 2-3 weeks for delivery.

www.ingramcontent.com/pod-product-compliance
Lightning Source LLC
Chambersburg PA
CBHW030528080526
44586CB00011B/359